# COVERT VIOLENCE

## The Secret Weapon of the Powerless

Jack Levin and Julie B. Wiest

BRISTOL
UNIVERSITY
PRESS

First published in Great Britain in 2023 by

Bristol University Press
University of Bristol
1-9 Old Park Hill
Bristol
BS2 8BB
UK
t: +44 (0)117 374 6645
e: bup-info@bristol.ac.uk

Details of international sales and distribution partners are available at bristoluniversitypress.co.uk

© Bristol University Press 2023

British Library Cataloguing in Publication Data
A catalogue record for this book is available from the British Library

ISBN 978-1-5292-3068-0 hardcover
ISBN 978-1-5292-3069-7 paperback
ISBN 978-1-5292-3070-3 ePub
ISBN 978-1-5292-3071-0 ePdf

The right of Jack Levin and Julie B. Wiest to be identified as authors of this work has been asserted by them in accordance with the Copyright, Designs and Patents Act 1988.

Cover design: Qube Design
Front cover image: Pixabay/StockSnap
Bristol University Press use environmentally responsible print partners.
Printed and bound in Great Britain by CPI Group (UK) Ltd, Croydon, CR0 4YY

FSC
www.fsc.org
MIX
Paper | Supporting
responsible forestry
FSC® C013604

# Contents

# List of Figures and Tables

## Figures

## Tables

# About the Authors

Jack Levin and Julie B. Wiest co-authored *The Allure of Premeditated Murder: Why Some People Plan to Kill* (2018, Rowman & Littlefield), as well as several peer-reviewed journal articles, editorials, and other contributions.

**Jack Levin** is Professor Emeritus in the Department of Sociology at Northeastern University, where he co-directs its Brudnick Center on Violence and Conflict. He has authored or co-authored more than 30 books, most recently *Extreme Killing: Understanding Serial and Mass Murder*, *The Will to Kill: Making Sense of Senseless Murder*, and *The Violence of Hate: Understanding Harmful Forms of Bias and Bigotry*. Dr. Levin has also published more than 250 articles and columns in professional journals, books, magazines, and newspapers, such as *The New York Times*, *London Sunday Times*, *Boston Globe*, *Dallas Morning News*, *Philadelphia Inquirer*, *Christian Science Monitor*, *Chicago Tribune*, *Washington Post*, and *USA Today*. Dr. Levin was honored by the Massachusetts Council for Advancement and Support of Education as its "Professor of the Year" and by the American Sociological Association for his contributions to the public understanding of sociology. He has also received awards from the Eastern Sociological Society, New England Sociological Association, Association of Clinical and Applied Sociology, Society for the Study of Social Problems, and Who's Who. Moreover, he has spoken to a wide variety of community, academic, and professional groups, including the White House Conference on Hate Crimes, the Department of Justice, OSCE's Office for Democratic Institutions and Human Rights, and the International Association of Chiefs of Police.

**Julie B. Wiest** is Professor of Sociology at West Chester University of Pennsylvania, where she teaches courses on culture, social psychology, and digital research/analytics. Her research primarily focuses on the sociocultural contexts of violence, mass media studies, and the relationship between new media technologies and social change. Dr. Wiest authored *Creating Cultural Monsters: Serial Murder in America* (2011, Taylor & Francis Group) and scholarly articles examining a variety of aspects related to public interest in and understandings of extreme violence, as well as the ways in which violence and crime are represented in both fiction and nonfiction mass media. She is Series Co-Editor of the *Interpretive Lenses in Sociology* book series (Bristol University Press, 2022—) and Senior Crime and Media Editor for the *Studies in Media and Communications* book series (Emerald Publishing, 2013—), for which she edited two volumes published in 2021: *Theorizing Criminality and Policing in the Digital Media Age* (Vol. 20) and *Mass Media Representations of Crime and Criminality* (Vol. 21).

# Acknowledgments

Thank you to the editorial and production teams at Bristol University Press for all their hard work, advice, and encouragement throughout the publication process. Thanks also to the scholars who reviewed our proposal, as their encouraging and constructive feedback helped us to further develop the book's primary concepts and arguments, and certainly enhanced its overall quality.

*Jack Levin*: I very much appreciate the feedback and encouragement I have received from colleagues at Northeastern University and elsewhere. I am especially thankful to criminologists Jamie Fox, Paul Iganski, and Jack McDevitt, as well as sociologists Arnie Arluke and Gordana Rabrenovic, with whom I have collaborated on many interesting projects in the past. I am also grateful to my wife, "Flea," for her enduring patience during the process of co-authoring this book, when instead we could have taken a vacation in the Bahamas with our wonderful grandchildren—Ben, Jaden, Ethan, Gavin, and Dan. Thank you sincerely.

*Julie B. Wiest*: I am most grateful for the longstanding love and support of my family and closest friends—Christian, Mom, Dan, Della, Dan C., Jackie, Anteaus, Jana, and Pamela—as well as my longtime mentors whose guidance and wisdom I never could repay, especially Betsy Morrow and Dr. Jerry Morrow, Dr. Suzanne Kurth, and Nancy Carroll. Thanks also to my research assistants, Hillary and Nell, and to my fantastic colleagues and friends who are a constant source of inspiration and encouragement, especially Tom, Laura, Myron, Shannon, Kylie, Carrie, Bessie, and Israel.

1

# An Introduction
# to Covert Violence, Power, and
# Social Institutions

Violent crime and sadistic behavior are often featured prominently in Western news and entertainment media. Many of these consumers, particularly in the United States, have become accustomed to reports of deadly school shootings, mass killings in public places like cinemas and shopping malls, and racist attacks inside community centers and houses of worship. Every day in cities and towns around the world, brutal gang warfare and acts of domestic violence tear at the fabric of social life. These types of violence are explicit, shocking, and often sensationalized, spreading fear throughout a community. They have also received plenty of attention from academics, journalists, members of law enforcement, and members of the public with an interest in crime and violent behavior.

*Covert violence*, on the other hand, is a type of everyday violence that exists deep in the shadows of society. Until now, these acts of murder, mischief, and mayhem have been mostly overlooked in academic and mainstream studies of criminal behavior. They are generally unnoticed by would-be victims, too—that is, until it is too late. Indeed, inconspicuousness is a common feature of these violent acts, and the perpetrators rely on others' inattention as they plot and prepare before striking surreptitiously and then slinking back under cover.

Most reported violence involves an *overt* act, or an explicit and aggressive encounter between offender(s) and victim(s). In contrast, property crimes tend to be *covert* acts in terms of the offenders' efforts to avoid detection and contact with victims. Most home break-ins occur in unoccupied dwellings, for example, and acts of vandalism are rarely committed in broad daylight. The clandestine aspect of covert violence defies this crime pattern, but its damage is just as devastating and potentially deadly as any other violent event. These acts of violence are committed by perpetrators who avoid drawing attention to themselves by maintaining a low profile and staying far away from the public spotlight. Not unlike many property offenses, covert acts of violence typically remain subterranean. Unlike many school shooters and rampage killers, those who commit covert violence—even deadly violence—are not interested in seeing their name in the news or their picture on the cover of *People* magazine. Unlike family annihilators who kill every member one by one before taking their own life, they don't seek recognition as a powerful head of a household. Unlike gang members who use deadly violence to terrorize their enemies and entire communities, they don't revel in a show of power. What most sets covert violence apart from nearly all other types is the passiveness of the actor's aggression.

Perpetrators of covert violence have a wide range of motives, use a variety of methods, and represent all ages, genders, races, and classes. One common characteristic of this unusual group of violent actors, however, is power—or, rather, *a lack of power*—though the context of any individual actor's powerlessness varies. Some perpetrators lack the physical ability to overpower their targets, while others are hampered by economic, political, or personal weakness. Yet they turn to covert violence because it provides the camouflage needed to overcome their powerlessness and successfully carry out their violent plans.

The animal kingdom is replete with examples of covert violence perpetrated by weaker, often diminutive, creatures that overpower much larger and stronger animals. Tiny insects such as Africanized bees and fire ants are capable of painful, sometimes fatal attacks on large mammals, including humans. Snakes can kill—and consume whole—large animals that far outweigh them, including deer, cattle, and even humans, as well as reptiles as large and ornery as a crocodile. Tarantulas commonly prey on animals many times their own size and weight, including some small mammals, but they are also the unexpected prey of some types of wasps (which are so good at killing the large, venomous spiders that the insects are also known as "tarantula hawks"). Even some web-building spiders have been known to feed on birds and bats that get stuck in their sticky traps. From the animal kingdom to human societies, covert violence is the secret weapon of the powerless.

Our focus in this book is on weak and powerless human perpetrators who seek to level the playing field by surreptitiously attacking more powerful targets when they least expect it, frequently in the dead of night, but always while their victims are unsuspecting. Because these perpetrators lack the physical, economic, political, or personal strength needed for a direct attack on their enemy, they choose to strike from the shadows and provide their own version of justice. When covert violence occurs with efficiency and competence, nothing is out of place, everything looks ordinary, and there is no indication that a profound act of violence is about to occur. There are no red flags, no warning signs, and no theater or drama beforehand or in the aftermath—only the terrible damage left behind and very few clues to solve the case. Although secrecy is a component of many violent acts—if only to avoid official detection and subsequent criminal punishment—acts of covert violence are distinct.

## Some data on deaths

According to Federal Bureau of Investigation (FBI) statistics, there were 16,425 homicides in the United States in 2019.[1] For 13,927 of those homicides, the FBI also collected additional details related to the perpetrators, victims, and circumstances, revealing, for example, that about 74 percent of those 13,927 homicides were committed with a firearm—a rifle, handgun, or shotgun—and another almost 11 percent were fatal stabbings. These figures make clear that, even without including additional overt methods, homicides committed via overt means make up the vast majority of U.S. homicide statistics.

   This conclusion is generally consistent with global homicide data, in fact, as the United Nations Office on Drugs and Crime data (UNODC, 2019) indicate that overt methods account for nearly all homicides worldwide. Of global homicides in 2017 (the most recent data available at the time of writing) with a known primary cause of death (those with an unknown cause accounted for just 5 percent of the total), firearms were used in 54 percent of cases, sharp objects (such as knives and swords) were used in 22 percent of cases, and some other mechanism (including poisoning, wielding a blunt object, and hand-to-hand combat) was used in 24 percent of cases (UNODC, 2019). Firearms accounted for a larger majority of homicides within most nations in the Americas, while sharp objects accounted for either a majority or the largest share of homicides in nations such as Austria, Canada, Guyana, Hungary, Poland, and Sweden; some other mechanism accounted for either a majority or the largest share of homicides in nations such as the Czech Republic, Latvia, Lithuania, Moldova, Romania, and the United Kingdom (UNODC, 2019). Yet, all these figures may only represent the visible and immediately countable portion of murder in a society, or those committed via *overt* methods. When covert criminals effectively commit acts of violence, however, the misdeeds may not appear in official statistics or even warrant informal scrutiny. Indeed, the casualties of covert violence may be classified as something else entirely. A closer look at U.S. death data helps to illustrate this possibility.

   Consider that, in the year 2019, the FBI reported 156 murders committed by strangulation or asphyxiation (about 1 percent of all homicides that year), 109 with poison or narcotics (less than 1 percent), 84 by fire or explosives (less than 1 percent), and seven by drowning (less than one-tenth of 1 percent).

**Table 1.1:** U.S. deaths by selected cause and manner, 2019

| Cause of death | Manner of death | | |
|---|---|---|---|
| | Homicide* | Accident** | Suicide** |
| Strangulation, hanging, and/or suffocation | 156 | 7,076 | 13,563 |
| Poisoning and/or exposure to noxious substances | 109 | 65,773 | 6,125 |
| Exposure to smoke, fire, and/or flames | 84 | 2,692 | – |
| Drowning and/or submersion | 7 | 3,692 | – |

  ★ *Based on data from the Federal Bureau of Investigation*

★★ *Based on data from the Centers for Disease Control and Prevention*


**Table 1.2:** U.S. deaths by manner, 2019

| | Number | % |
|---|---|---|
| Natural causes (diseases, illnesses, and other conditions) | 2,599,682 | 91.06 |
| Unintentional injuries (accidents) | 173,040 | 6.06 |
| Suicides (intentional self-harm) | 47,511 | 1.66 |
| Assault (homicide)** | 19,141 | 0.67 |
| Complications of medical and surgical care | 5,329 | 0.19 |
| Legal intervention (deaths in the course of law enforcement) | 652 | 0.02 |
| **Total deaths*** | **2,854,838** | **100.0** |

  ★ *Based on data from the Centers for Disease Control and Prevention*

★★ *CDC data and FBI data on annual homicides often do not match because the former is a medical determination related to manner of death, while the latter is a legal determination*


Yet, all of these are common causes of accidental death in the United States, and two are frequent methods of suicide (see Table 1.1). The Centers for Disease Control and Prevention (CDC) recorded 173,040 deaths from unintentional injuries in 2019 (Xu et al., 2021; see Table 1.2). Of that total, 65,773—nearly 40 percent of all accidental deaths that year—were poisonings; another 7,076 deaths were recorded as accidental strangulation/ suffocation, 3,692 were drownings, and 2,692 were from exposure to fire/ smoke. Moreover, strangulation/suffocation and poisoning are frequent methods of suicide, which is the 10th-leading cause of death in the United States (accidents rank third, after heart disease and cancer; see Xu et al., 2021). Of the 47,511 suicides recorded in 2019 by the CDC, 13,563 were completed by strangulation/suffocation, and 6,125 were by poisoning.

Because people rarely commit suicide in the presence of witnesses, however, the exact circumstances leading to such a death are not necessarily certain. Further, as most Americans die from natural causes (accounting for at least 90 percent of the annual total), it seems worth considering that fatal poisonings—whether by accident, suicide, or homicide—can appear identical to deaths from illness or disease.

We will likely never know how many of the fatal accidents, suicides, and naturally caused deaths recorded each year are really overlooked acts of covert violence. This possible reality has received very little scholarly or other professional consideration so far. Farrell (2019, p. 2) raised alarm about the "likely underestimated prevalence of serial poisoning" and indicated that it is not unusual to ultimately discover "more killings than expected" after serial poisoners have been identified. In addition, a short article was recently published in a medical journal with the relevant title "A homicide in disguise" (Khurshid et al., 2022). It recounts the circumstances surrounding a Pakistani death investigation that was initially ruled an accidental drowning, but later found to be a homicide by strangulation. The authors concluded in part that:

> Drowning may be a means to disguise homicide. The culprit may dispose of the body in the water and set the crime scene up as a suicide attempt or an accident. Therefore, medicolegal autopsies play a crucial role to rule out foul play in skeptical deaths to find the culprit. (Khurshid et al., 2022)

This appears to support—or perhaps even warn about—the likelihood of additional such cases.

Similarly, the findings from our exploratory study of fatal covert violence in the United States suggest that there may be far more instances than anyone has previously indicated, and they also provide some preliminary clues about the perpetrators, victims, and circumstances of these vicious attacks. What is most apparent is that the surreptitious character of these acts serves to conceal them from official sources of law enforcement. As a result, there may be much larger numbers of certain "passive-aggressive" offenses than are recognized in official data collected by law enforcement agencies around the country. In extreme cases, we might never recognize that a death was more than a result of natural causes or an unfortunate accident.

## An exploratory study of reclassified U.S. deaths

Studying covert violence poses some unique challenges, as its successful commission means that it has not been recognized for what it is. Rather, the harm caused by a covert act of violence, once detected, would be attributed to some other cause or some other actor. Indeed, covert methods can conceal intentional violence and prevent the apprehension of offenders for long periods of time, or perhaps indefinitely in some cases. On occasion, though, a covert act of violence may eventually be revealed for what it is, and examining such cases sheds light on the murky circumstances of these offenses.

Using the Nexis database of newspapers and newswires across the United States, we collected every case we could find over a three-year period (June 2017 to July 2020) in which a death that was originally classified as something other than homicide was subsequently reclassified as a homicide. In all, our sample includes 37 cases, one of which had two perpetrators and several of which included multiple victims, for a total of 38 perpetrators (one whose identity was unknown) and 53 victims. Despite the sample being limited to reclassified cases that had received news media attention, uncovering an average of one case per month across the study timeframe was an unexpectedly large number.[2] Moreover, the cases included homicides that had been committed across a wide timespan—from 1975 to 2019—and in all regions of the country. During the three-year period under study, these cases were in varying stages of investigation, adjudication, or legal resolution, but all had been officially reclassified as homicides.

Most of the weapons employed by the covert killers in our sample differed sharply from what is reflected in FBI murder statistics (see Table 1.3). Notably, of the 53 fatalities in our sample, there was only one fatal shooting and just two stabbing deaths. Instead, the covert killers overwhelmingly used more passive-aggressive approaches: 11 victims (21 percent) were fatally poisoned, eight victims (15 percent) were drowned, eight more (15 percent) were suffocated or smothered, seven (13 percent) died by blunt force or beating, four (7.5 percent) were strangled or hanged, and another four (7.5 percent) died in fires. The causes of the remaining eight victims' deaths were either unknown or unclear, including one case in which an infant was left for dead in a ditch.

Leaving only ambiguous signals as to the cause of each death, the methods employed by the covert killers in our sample were clearly effective in throwing investigators and medical practitioners off the track, at least initially (see Table 1.4). Just six of the 37 total cases (16 percent) were originally classified as undetermined, with more than one third (14 cases, or 37 percent) counted as accidental deaths, ten cases (26 percent) as illness/natural causes, seven cases (18 percent) as missing persons, and one case (3 percent) as suicide.

The overwhelming majority of our cases—just over three quarters of the sample—took several months to multiple years before they were officially recognized as homicides. Only nine (about 24 percent) were reclassified as homicides within a matter of weeks or days. The median time between original classification and reclassification for the cases in our sample was 13 years, and the longest amount of time was 44 years. What led to each reclassification varied, but some clear patterns emerged in our sample. Most of the cases (nearly 60 percent) were spurred by an ongoing or additional

**Table 1.3:** U.S. homicides by method

| Out of cases where method is known | Overall rate (%)* | Covert rate (%)** |
|---|---|---|
| Shooting | 73.7 | 2.0 |
| Stabbing | 10.6 | 4.0 |
| Blunt force/beating | 7.2 | 13.0 |
| Unknown/undetermined/other | 6.0 | 15.0 |
| Poisoning/narcotics | 0.8 | 21.0 |
| Suffocation/smothering | 0.7 | 15.0 |
| Fire/explosives | 0.6 | 7.5 |
| Strangulation | 0.5 | 7.5 |
| Drowning | 0.1 | 15.0 |

\* *Based on 2019 FBI data of 13,927 homicides*

\*\* *Based on authors' study of 53 deaths that occurred 1975–2019 and were reclassified as homicides between July 2017 and June 2020*

**Table 1.4:** Classification and reclassification of covert homicides

| Original classification of death | % |
|---|---|
| Accidental death | 37 |
| Illness/natural causes | 26 |
| Missing person | 18 |
| Undetermined | 16 |
| Suicide | 3 |
| **Time to reclassification*** | **%** |
| Days | 16 |
| Weeks | 8 |
| Months | 26 |
| Years | 50 |
| **Impetus for reclassification** | **%** |
| New witness or evidence found/ ongoing investigation | 58 |
| Encouragement by family/friend | 29 |
| Additional incident raised suspicion | 13 |

Note: There are 38 homicides within the 37 cases, as one involved two distinct acts of covert murder that occurred 13 years apart and under substantially different circumstances.

\* *Measured as the time between each death's original classification and reclassification as homicide: days (up to 14 days), weeks (15 days to three months), months (more than three months up to two years), or years (more than two years)*

investigation, particularly when a new witness came forward, new evidence was uncovered, or advances in evidence testing allowed for new results. The next most common reason that subsequently reclassified cases were given another look—accounting for about 30 percent of the cases—was the urging of a suspicious community member, often a family member or friend of the victim. The remaining cases were re-examined either because the perpetrator was caught committing an act of additional violence that raised suspicion about previous events or because the perpetrator eventually confessed.

These results strongly suggest that covert acts of violence may have been significantly under-represented in official reports of criminal homicide. When an intentional smothering, for example, is regarded by a medical examiner as death by natural causes, then the homicidal ending of a life may never be properly recorded as murder. When poisoning is viewed by investigators as the result of a terminal illness or accidental ingestion of a deadly substance, then that death is being treated as a benign incident rather than a malignant act of murder. Covert criminals are adept at operating under the radar, steering an investigation in the wrong direction and saving themselves from suspicion and eventual apprehension—for many years, if not forever.

In addition to the stark differences between characteristics of homicides as reported in official statistics and within our sample, our study results also sharply diverge from FBI data on the demographic characteristics of perpetrators and victims, as well as the killers' motives for murder. Gender differences are particularly notable (see Table 1.5), as official data show that homicide—like most acts of violence—is a male-dominated crime. According to FBI data, only about 12 percent of all perpetrators and just under a quarter (21.5 percent) of victims are female. Yet, those figures may be far higher—possibly double—when it comes to covert cases of homicide. In our sample, about one third (32.4 percent) of perpetrators and nearly half (49 percent) of victims were female—far higher representations than in official statistics. It appears that more benignly regarded covert homicide may involve far more female perpetrators *and* female victims, compared to more recognized, overt types of homicide.

Regarding victims' age, our study results contrast the most with official homicide data for those in the most vulnerable age groups (see Table 1.6).

**Table 1.5:** U.S. homicide perpetrators and victims by gender

| Out of cases where gender is known | Overall rate (%)★ | Covert rate (%)★★ |
| --- | --- | --- |
| Female perpetrators | 12.0 | 32.4 |
| Female victims | 21.5 | 49.0 |

★ *Based on 2019 FBI data of 11,743 known perpetrators and 13,899 victims with known data*

★★ *Based on authors' study of deaths that occurred 1975–2019 and were reclassified as homicides between July 2017 and June 2020 with 37 identified perpetrators and 53 total victims*

**Table 1.6:** U.S. homicide victims by age

| Out of cases with known information | Overall rate (%)* | Covert rate (%)** |
| --- | --- | --- |
| Victims ages 12 or younger | 4.1 | 26.4 |
| Victims ages 75 or older | 2.0 | 17.0 |

\* Based on 2019 FBI data of 13,927 victims with known data

\*\* Based on authors' study of deaths that occurred 1975–2019 and were reclassified as homicides between July 2017 and June 2020 with 53 total victims

**Table 1.7:** The relationship between U.S. homicide perpetrators and victims

| | Overall rate (%)* | Covert rate (%)** |
| --- | --- | --- |
| Relationship is unknown | 51.1 | 1.9 |
| **Out of cases where relationship is known** | | |
| Perpetrator is family member (includes spouse/domestic partner) | 25.4 | 61.5 |
| Perpetrator is known to victim (includes friend, boyfriend/girlfriend, acquaintance, co-worker, etc.) | 55.3 | 32.7 |
| Perpetrator and victim are strangers | 19.3 | 5.8 |

\* Based on 2019 FBI data of 13,927 homicides

\*\* Based on authors' study of deaths that occurred 1975–2019 and were reclassified as homicides between July 2017 and June 2020 with 37 identified perpetrators and 53 total victims

Official statistics show that Americans on opposite ends of the age spectrum—the youngest and oldest—are the least likely victims of homicide by age group. Indeed, FBI data show that only about 4 percent of U.S. homicide victims are 12 years or younger, and just 2 percent are 75 years or older. However, our sample of reclassified homicides revealed far higher levels of victims in these vulnerable age groups, which combined accounted for more than 40 percent of all victims.

Another difference between official homicide data and our results relates to the relationship between perpetrators and victims (see Table 1.7). It is important to first note that in about half of homicides represented in FBI reports, the perpetrator–victim relationship is unknown (compared to just one case out of 37 in our sample). Of cases with known information, FBI data indicate that nearly 20 percent of homicides are between strangers, while 25 percent are committed by family members and the remaining 55 percent involve other people who are known to one another (for example, friend, boyfriend/girlfriend, acquaintance, co-worker, neighbor, and so on). In our sample, just over 60 percent of the homicides were committed by family

**Table 1.8:** U.S. homicides by motive

|  | Overall rate (%)★ | Covert rate (%)★★ |
|---|---|---|
| Motive is unknown | 41.2 | 27.0 |
| **Out of cases where motive is known** | | |
| Felony murder*** | 24.6 | – |
| Argument/conflict | 44.2 | 25.9 |
| Other | 31.2 | 14.8 |
| Profit | – | 44.4 |
| Pleasure/sadism/power | – | 11.1 |
| Revenge | – | 3.7 |

★ *Based on 2019 FBI data of 13,927 homicides*

★★ *Based on authors' study of 37 cases (some with multiple victims) in which deaths that occurred 1975–2019 were reclassified as homicides between July 2017 and June 2020*

*** *Felony murder includes deaths that occurred in conjunction with the commission of another felony crime (rape, robbery, burglary, etc.)*

members, about one third by other perpetrators who knew their victims, and less than 10 percent (just three cases) by strangers. This suggests that covert violence disproportionately involves perpetrators and victims who are known to one another or—even more likely—are intimately acquainted.

Lastly, motives appear to diverge for those who employ overt versus covert methods (see Table 1.8). Although motivations for murder are notoriously difficult to determine (and, thus, were categorized as unknown in 41 percent of cases in FBI data and 27 percent of cases in our sample), some insights still can be gleaned. Out of the overall U.S. cases in FBI statistics with a known motive, the largest proportion (about 44 percent) occurred during an argument or personal conflict. These circumstances tend to be easier to understand than other motives for murder, as they include so-called "crimes of passion" and encompass well-known terms (and TV show titles) like "snapped." Tempers flare. Verbal insults between family members or friends escalate into physical violence. And the situation is often made worse by the presence of alcohol and/or drugs. An additional 25 percent of FBI-reported homicides occurred during the commission of another felony, such as sexual assault, robbery, or burglary. For the covert homicides with a known motive in our sample, in contrast, nearly 45 percent were motivated by profit, with most of these relating to anticipated collections of life insurance or inheritance. Compared to 44 percent of FBI homicides, only about one quarter of the covert murders occurred because of anger or loss of control. This suggests that homicides in our study were disproportionately less likely than official nationwide reports to be fueled by spontaneous passion and more likely to occur as planned attacks for money.

The results of our study offer a glimpse into the magnitude of covert violence and its consequences. Each case in the sample is an example of a *murder* that for some amount of time—more than a decade, on average—was officially recorded as an accidental, natural, self-inflicted, or undetermined death. Uncovering 37 of these cases in an arbitrary 36-month timeframe is nothing short of stunning. Although it's impossible to know how many total murders were misidentified within the 45-year period represented by the sample cases (from 1975 to 2019), it's reasonable to assume that such errors are infrequently detected. Official medical and legal determinations are rarely revisited (when they are, professional egos and courtesies tend to prevail), and cold-case deaths are notoriously difficult to solve (in the rare instances when limited resources even allow for continuing investigation).

Even when suspicions are raised, covert methods for murder can be very difficult to prove. An alert medical examiner, for example, might notice the telltale smell of bitter almonds to diagnose a death by cyanide poisoning, but their ability to rule it a homicide or a suicide could be impossible without an eyewitness, visual recording, or other concrete evidence. In contrast, stabbing deaths are nearly always clear homicides, and details related to entry and exit wounds in most fatal shootings can distinguish between murder and suicide. Thus, we suggest that our sample of reclassified homicides is likely a *subset of a subset* of misidentified murder cases, representing only the portion that was both officially recognized *and* covered in the news media during the study timeframe. And this does not even address *attempted* murders that have been classified as illnesses, accidental injuries, and suicide attempts. Although no data currently exist that provide reliable estimates or valid guidance, it is certainly possible that there are far more instances of extreme covert violence in the United States (and around the world) than anyone has dared to imagine.

## Power and social institutions

The uneven distribution of power in social institutions—from families and schools to workplaces, healthcare, and mass media—casts wide shadows that conceal both the advantages of power and the disadvantages of powerlessness. This allows members of powerful groups to enjoy important advantages (that are frequently unearned and/or unacknowledged) while comfortably ignoring the (typically undeserved) suffering of the powerless. At the same time, these powerful group members may struggle to even recognize the advantages they hold—advantages that tend to be glaringly obvious to those who don't have them. Moreover, both advantages and disadvantages tend to compound over time, resulting in an ever-growing gap between those with the most advantages, who sit at the "top" of the social hierarchy, and those with the fewest advantages, who sit at the "bottom." This trend toward increasing inequality over time—which is typically determined using data on average income and educational attainment—is most pronounced in low-income nations, but also exists in most economies around the world (Narayan et al., 2018). Indeed, income inequality in the United States has increased in recent decades, maintains that trajectory, and is the highest among Group of Seven (G7) nations, followed in order by the United Kingdom, Italy, Japan, Canada, Germany, and France (Horowitz et al., 2020).

As an illustration, the distributions of both income and wealth in the United States consistently show very little change across the average American's lifetime (see Pew Charitable Trusts, 2012). This is especially true for those at the two extremes—the top 20 percent and the bottom 20 percent of families in terms of income and wealth—where the family income and wealth of the average adult is most likely to mirror that of the household in which they were raised. In other words, wealthy families tend to stay wealthy across generations, and poor families tend to stay poor. This is not a coincidence or fluke; instead, it demonstrates that family socioeconomic status spawns hidden advantages and disadvantages that tend to reproduce themselves over time.

Unseen advantages and disadvantages are linked to virtually all social statuses and affect people's experiences across all social institutions. The result is differential access to social power, which can be understood as a person's ability to live as they individually choose and/or a person's ability to control the way other people live. In general, power is a necessary element for accomplishing overt acts, particularly those that may have negative consequences for others. Although a thorough discussion of social power and its dimensions is beyond the scope of this book, it is useful to distinguish between legitimate and illegitimate forms. For example, the company boss who fires an employee or the professor who requires a disruptive student to leave their classroom uses legitimate power (also known as *authority*), but illegitimate power also can be effective, as in the case of a robber who wields a weapon to compel someone to hand over their wallet.

When people lack power, they more often find themselves controlled by others, lacking the autonomy to *overtly* do and say what they please. To be clear, autonomy and power do not exist in some objective reality. It is possible that a person who feels powerless might actually be capable of overt action, yet the feeling of powerlessness is likely to prevent an attempt to act. In this sense, the influence of power in covert violence centers more on *feelings* of power, or *perceptions* of autonomy, from the would-be perpetrator's perspective. Concepts in persuasion theory such as *self-efficacy* and *perceived behavioral control* (see Ajzen, 1991; Bandura, 1991; O'Keefe and Medway, 1997) emphasize that most human action is predicated on the actor's perceived ability to successfully perform the action in question. This aligns with classical sociological theorizing on the social construction of reality (see Berger and Luckmann, 1966), including the well-known Thomas Theorem that states: "If (people) define situations as real, they are real in their consequences" (Thomas and Thomas, 1928).

Three types of power are emphasized here—physical, economic, and personal—each of which is described briefly next, but more thoroughly in subsequent chapters. *Physical power* may relate to actual physical strength and/or stature (for example, one person being larger and stronger than someone else) or it may relate to the size of one group compared to another (for example, one nation's army outnumbering that of its opponent). Other social dynamics are linked to physical power, such as gender and age. Men tend to be physically bigger and stronger on average compared to women, for example. Although both biological and sociological explanations for gender differences are debated, it is clear that men's greater-on-average capacity to physically overpower women is exponentially more dangerous when combined with traditional gender roles that legitimate male aggression while encouraging female submission. The origin of increased danger applies to would-be victims of any gender, as boys and men are not just the most common perpetrators of interpersonal violence, but are also the most common victims of all types except for sexual violence. In the neighborhood or schoolyard, for example, the smaller and weaker boys are common victims of bullies who tend to be big and strong. In some cases, a lack of physical power is related to the youth of a target, such as some victims of older bullies and children who are weaker than their adult tormenters. Yet, plenty of physically weaker perpetrators have successfully used covert violence to attack a much stronger target of their wrath.

*Economic power* relates to one's ability to obtain and utilize valuable social goods. In a capitalist society, economic power equates most clearly to one's access to capital, or the complement of one's net assets. This form of power is influential in all aspects of U.S. life, but its role in covert violence is most visible within families and the workplace. There are plenty of examples of people who plan—and some who carry out—the death of a family member in hopes of receiving a big insurance or inheritance payout, and financial inequalities in the workplace can cause tensions that occasionally lead to violence.

*Personal power* describes an individual's ability to control the manner and direction of their own life, as well as to receive the respect and acknowledgment from others that they feel they deserve. The desire for this kind of power is strongest in individualistic societies (such as the United States) compared to more collectivistic ones, but it is also influenced by cultural expectations about *who* deserves power, *how much* power a person should have, and what constitutes *legitimate expressions* of power. Links between personal power and covert violence—especially among Americans—are most evident in the social institutions of education, politics and government, mass media, and healthcare.

Importantly, relationships between powerlessness and covert violence appear to vary across different social institutions—albeit in patterned ways. For example, physically powerless actors are more likely to strike using covert methods within the contexts of family and close relationships, formal education, or politics and government. Those lacking economic means are more likely to engage in covert violence within the family and close relationships or the workplace. People who feel ignored, unheard, or otherwise denied the recognition, consideration, or autonomy to which they feel entitled (akin to a deficit of personal power) are more likely to attack clandestinely in situations related to formal education, politics and government, the mass media, or healthcare. In other words, different *kinds* of power operate differently in different social institutions. Thus, a deficit of one kind of power may be more or less meaningful—and more or less likely to induce covert violence—in one situation compared to another. Each subsequent chapter, then, focuses on one social institution to examine the influence of powerlessness most relevant to the patterns of covert violence found there.[3]

Although this book focuses on covert acts of violence committed by powerless perpetrators, that is not to suggest that members of powerful groups are excluded from such behavior. Powerful actors do engage in covert violence on occasion, but these acts are far more attractive to the powerless, who otherwise have few (or no) opportunities for overt action. An infamous example is English physician Harold F. Shipman, nicknamed "Dr. Death," who was convicted in January 2000 of murdering 15 patients between 1975 and 1998 (and suspected in the cases of many more patient deaths). He would administer a lethal dose of medication—usually the powerful opioid diamorphine—to some of his elderly patients and then sign their death certificates (indicating old age as the cause) and falsify medical records to reflect a trajectory of failing health. Shipman went to great lengths to hide his deadly deeds over a period of 33 years, but his attempts to disguise them as something else entirely—something nonviolent and natural—is what distinguishes his acts as covert violence.

Powerful actors generally have greater access than their powerless counterparts to the means necessary for hiding or covering up overt acts of violence. Indeed, many overtly violent actors keep their plans hidden before implementation (frequently for practical reasons, such as to avoid the discovery/foiling of the intended act or to benefit from the element of surprise) and/or attempt to conceal the fact that anything at all occurred (for example, by disposing of a body, cleaning up a crime scene, erasing surveillance video, etc.)—but the violent act itself is generally revealed to the target and/or others present, even if just seconds beforehand. Powerful perpetrators also may possess enough financial and/or other resources to convince witnesses or co-conspirators to remain silent about what they know. And, if all else fails, they can typically afford the kind of legal representation needed for the best chance of acquittal.

Rather than merely covering up an act of violence and/or a perpetrator's role in it, however, covert violence is meant to be concealed during the entire timeframe—in the planning phase, the implementation, and the aftermath—and from *everyone*, including the target. Overtly violent actors may attempt to hide their own culpability in the act (while making little or no attempt to conceal the *violence* itself), but covertly violent actors attempt to disguise the act as something *nonviolent*. In other words, if overt actors *hide*, then covert actors could be characterized as *hiding in plain sight*. Covert acts of violence are *not* usually the crimes that make the front page of the daily newspaper or the cover of *People* magazine.

## Social contexts of aggression and violence

Social psychologists have known for decades that certain individuals tend to lash out in anger when, in their view, an important goal is blocked and they are prevented from achieving what they desire. Not everyone who becomes frustrated by the disappointments of everyday life reacts with violence, of course; many simply try again, accept their fate, or lower their aspirations. But some frustrated individuals become angry enough to claim a measure of personal justice, which they believe has been denied them through official channels. In these cases, the method of retaliation is often violent, either physical or psychological, and the source of their frustrations is typically the intended target—but not always.

Tempers frequently flair on the roadways in and out of major cities during afternoon rush hour. Commuters who are anxious to get home after a long day at work may feel pangs of frustration from the gridlock alone or perhaps from the perceived rudeness or unfair treatment of other drivers. Most will express their frustrations by honking the horn, yelling an obscenity, or perhaps wildly gesturing. A few might leave their vehicles to confront another driver, and occasionally a confrontation will turn into a fistfight or shootout on the side of the highway or at a busy intersection

The workplace is another primary arena for frustration-aggression. Consider the case of workplace vengeance in which an employee is fired and then returns to get even with the boss through the barrel of a gun. Or perhaps a worker was passed over for a promotion or denied a raise and then decides to open fire on his colleagues. Such episodes of vengeful violence frequently make the national headlines and cable news, particularly when such brutality leads to fatalities, and these perpetrators are almost always captured—or killed, either by their own hand or by police.

In some cases, vengeful workers feel powerless to enact their ideal revenge against an unjust boss or uncaring co-workers. Instead, they might look for a "scapegoat," directing their anger at a more vulnerable target such as their spouse or child, a family pet or wild animal, or a subordinate in the workplace who lacks the capacity to strike back. In the wider society, racial prejudice and discrimination are often regarded as a form of displaced aggression. Innocent members of racial and religious minority groups, as well as others with subordinate social status, are too often the victims of frustrated individuals looking for someone safe to blame for their lifetime of disappointments.

These explanations for violent acts of vengeance have enjoyed longtime popularity in both scholarly and mainstream accounts of criminality. Perhaps the most famous is the psychological Frustration-Aggression Hypothesis, originally offered by John Dollard and colleagues (1939) and further developed by Neal E. Miller and colleagues (1941) and later by Leonard Berkowitz (1969), among others. Fundamentally, the theory explains aggressive behavior as one possible outcome of the frustration experienced from interference with one's goals. Many people can likely relate to an urge to lash out against someone who has wronged them, even if few actually do so.

Within sociology, classic strain theories (for example, Cloward and Ohlin, 1966; Merton, 1968; Cohen, 1971) explain deviant behavior as a possible response to the stress experienced when structural inequalities prevent people from achieving culturally valued goals via socially legitimate means. For example, someone born into a low-income U.S. family who has limited access to quality education and job prospects but who is also committed to the idealistic notion of the "American dream" may decide that, in lieu of earning minimum wage at a "legitimate" job, they will instead find their own way to make money. There are many ways to earn a living in resource-poor communities that are not technically legal, of course, and some are quite innovative (for example, producing and selling duplicated media products or knock-off luxury goods, or selling cigarettes individually from a pack).

Later criminologists (especially Agnew, 1992; Messner and Rosenfeld, 1994/2013) made substantial headway in developing the explanatory scope of these theories. In particular, the General Strain Theory incorporated negative emotions as an intermediary between experiencing strain and the likelihood of crime. Fundamentally, it explains that strain increases crime because the experience of stress can lead to negative feelings (such as anger, fear, and frustration), with which some people cope via criminal behavior—especially when social circumstances limit their legitimate options for coping. General Strain Theory also incorporates a range of additional strain types (for example, subjective and objective strains, and vicarious and anticipated strains) and explains how each type relates to individual social circumstances and the likelihood for crime commission. Many scholars have further developed these theories and have applied them in a variety of contexts and to a range of different groups (for a thorough overview of strain theories, see Agnew and Brezina [2010]).

Also relevant to this frustration-focused theoretical group is the social psychological concept of "crimes of resistance" (see Rios, 2012), which suggests that members of marginalized and/or criminalized communities sometimes commit petty crimes, such as shoplifting items of insignificant value or engaging in senseless acts of vandalism, as a way to express resistance to the oppressive powers that keep them from succeeding in mainstream society. In lieu of lashing out against the "powers that be," these actors exert their own autonomy and dignity through deliberate, albeit irrational, action. Crimes of resistance also provide a means for those actors to visibly object to their repeated mistreatment while simultaneously rejecting the authority of those involved in perpetuating systems of social inequality.

Somewhat similarly, the criminological concept of "inter-criminal victimization"—which also most commonly occurs within economically disadvantaged communities (Treadwell et al., 2020)—provides additional explanatory support for the relationship between feelings of powerlessness and criminal behavior for some actors. Unlike crimes of resistance, however, which typically target law-abiding victims (as symbols of the social power of which the perpetrator feels deprived), inter-criminal victimization refers to offenses in which both perpetrator(s) and victim(s) are criminals—though not necessarily involved in the same criminal enterprise. For example, a violent gangster might take an opportunity to rob a drug dealer, or a drug dealer might burglarize the home of a sex trafficker. Because these crimes occur among criminals and therefore no means for lawful recourse or compensation typically exist, a cycle of frustration and aggression is likely to develop that frequently results in a series of retaliatory violence. This is especially likely when retaliation is prescribed within the so-called "street culture" as an accepted—or perhaps expected—form of "street justice" (Jacobs and Wright, 1999, 2006). Indeed, the norms related to inter-criminal victimization have been found to differ among U.S. drug dealers, for whom retaliatory violence is virtually inevitable (Jacobs and Wright, 2006), and their U.K. counterparts, who appear to rarely engage in violent retaliation after being robbed or extorted by a rival (Treadwell et al., 2020).

Although the utility of frustration-aggression theories is debatable, whatever explanatory power they offer for violent behavior tends to be limited to conventional understandings of the concept (that is, *overt* violence). In the scholarly and professional literature (see Greydanus et al., 2021), aggression is typically divided into two types: direct and indirect. *Direct aggression* includes physical attacks (pushing, hitting, punching, yielding a weapon, etc.), as well as verbal abuse and threats of harm (which could include physical, emotional, financial, or other types of harm), that clearly target a person, a group of people, or an identity group (based on race, religion, nationality, gender, sexuality, age, etc.). *Indirect aggression* includes behaviors that promote the exclusion of the targeted person/group from social interactions and/or activities, including speaking negatively about them to others, spreading false information, socially isolating or disregarding them, and other circuitous actions. The scholarly literature is replete with explanations for aggression, but most can be categorized as based in biology or in social psychology (see Bushman, 2017).

*Violence* is broadly understood as a type of direct aggression—typically physical in form but not necessarily—that appears to be both impulsive and excessive (Greydanus et al., 2021). It is unclear, however, why there appears to be no corresponding concept for indirect aggression, which certainly could also occur in impulsive and excessive states. The concept of "indirect violence" exists, to be sure, but it is not linked to indirect aggression in the way that violence is typically linked to direct aggression (that is, it does not mean "a type of indirect aggression that appears to be both impulsive and excessive").

An early use of the term "indirect violence" is found in the medical literature to describe moderate to severe injuries sustained in trips, falls, or other mundane accidents (for example, Hermel and Gershon-Cohen, 1953; Bostman and Hanninen, 1982; Jones, 1902). Another use describes violence that is perpetrated by groups or institutions (for example, Balcells, 2011) rather than by individuals, which is similar to another concept called "structural violence" (for example, Farmer, 1996; Vorobej, 2008). Perhaps the most common use of the term in contemporary scholarly literature describes witnessing violent acts committed against others, with most such studies focusing on the psychological, mental, and/or emotional effects (for example, Romero-Daza et al., 2005; Shukla and Wiesner, 2015; Gollub et al., 2019).

Although the concept of *covert violence* is rooted in the theoretical concepts just reviewed, it is not described or explained by any of them. Rather, it is a distinct concept that explains the kinds of violent acts that otherwise might have been understood as "indirect-aggressive violence" or perhaps "passive-aggressive violence," but that are also characterized by multiple layers of secrecy. Indeed, some acts of covert violence are so competently veiled and executed that it may never be certain whether they were intentionally committed at all. Even when all other possibilities have been ruled out, there is often still lingering doubt as to the cause of the incident. Was it an accident? The work of a deranged but unknown stranger? Just a hoax? Despite the damage caused by these incidents and the difficulty of solving them, no existing theories have explained their causes—or offered effective ways to reduce their incidence—until now.

## Notes

[1] The year 2019 was selected for two primary reasons: (1) because it is the most recent year in which finalized data for both the CDC and the FBI were available, and (2) because it better represents ordinary circumstances before the COVID-19 pandemic disrupted everyday life around the world.

[2] A methodological note: the primary concepts and arguments presented in Chapter 1 are based on an exploratory study that consisted of a small sample size (37 cases), a narrow timeframe (three years), an exclusive focus on U.S. cases, and a potentially nonrepresentative sample (that is, only qualifying cases that received mainstream news coverage were included, though any reclassification of a death thought to be from some noncriminal manner to homicide is likely to be considered newsworthy). However, limiting a study timeframe and geographic focus are two methods for addressing issues arising from a small sample size and the possibility of a nonrepresentative sample, as they increase the likelihood of homogeneity—and thus comparability—of sample cases. Supplementing the study's findings are additional exemplar cases, as well as comparisons to data on overt violence and nonviolent causes of U.S. deaths. It is also important to acknowledge that most truly novel ideas begin with a narrow focus and limited cases that develop over time as they are investigated and applied in new ways and through different perspectives. As such, we hope this book inspires a new path toward knowledge building, and we encourage interested scholars and other professionals to use our concepts and arguments as a guide for examining the relationships among covert violence, power, and social institutions within other countries, cultures, and contexts. Our work is ongoing in these areas, too, as there is still much to learn about this long-overlooked type of violence before such shadowy acts can be fully brought into the light.

[3] The chapters focusing on politics and government (Chapter 5) and on mass media (Chapter 7) approach the concept of covert violence somewhat differently from the others, primarily because of fundamental differences in the composition of, and practices within, those social institutions that also differentiate most people's experiences within them. In particular, most people have only vicarious or passive experience with politics/government and traditional forms of mass media in their society, while it is likely for them to have direct experience within the institutions of family, formal education, the workplace, and/or healthcare (particularly for those in Western societies).

## References

Agnew, R. (1992). Foundation for a general strain theory of crime and delinquency. *Criminology, 30*(1), 47–88.

Agnew, R., and Brezina, T. (2010). Strain theories. In E. McLaughlin and T. Newburn (eds.), *The Sage handbook of criminological theory* (pp 96–113). Sage.

Ajzen, I. (1991). The theory of planned behavior. *Organizational Behavior and Human Decision Processes, 50*, 179–211.

Balcells, L. (2011). Continuation of politics by two means: direct and indirect violence in civil war. *Journal of Conflict Resolution, 55*(3), 397–422. https://doi.org/10.1177%2F0022002711400865

Bandura, A. (1991). Social cognitive theory of self-regulation. *Organizational Behavior and Human Decision Processes, 50*, 248–287.

Berger, P.L., and Luckmann, T. (1966). *The social construction of reality: A treatise in the sociology of knowledge.* Doubleday & Company.

Berkowitz, L. (1969). *Roots of aggression: A re-examination of the frustration-aggression hypothesis.* Atherton Press.

Bostman, O., and Hanninen, A. (1982). The fibular reciprocal fracture in tibial shaft fractures caused by indirect violence. *Archives of Orthopaedic and Traumatic Surgery, 100,* 115–121.

Bushman, B.J. (ed.) (2017). *Aggression and violence: A social psychological perspective.* Routledge.

Cloward, R.A., and Ohlin, L.E. (1966). *Delinquency and opportunity: A theory of delinquent gangs.* Free Press.

Cohen, A.K. (1971). *Delinquent boys: The culture of the gang.* Free Press.

Dollard, J., Miller, N.E., Doob, L.W., Mowrer, O.H., and Sears, R.R. (1939). *Frustration and aggression.* Yale University Press.

Farmer, P. (1996). On suffering and structural violence: A view from below. *Daedalus, 125*(1), 261–283.

Farrell, M. (2019). *Criminology of serial poisoners.* Palgrave Macmillan.

Gollub, E.L., Green, J., Richardson, L., Kaplan, I., and Shervington, D. (2019). Indirect violence exposure and mental health symptoms among an urban public-school population: Prevalence and correlates. *PLoS ONE, 14*(11). https://doi.org/10.1371/journal.pone.0224499

Greydanus, D.E., Hawver, J.R., and Rowland, D.C. (2021). Concepts of aggression: Perspectives in the 21st century. *Journal of Alternative Medicine Research, 13*(4), 361–385.

Hermel, M.B., and Gershon-Cohen, J. (1953). The nutcracker fracture of the cuboid by indirect violence. *Radiology, 60*(6), 850–854. https://doi.org/10.1148/60.6.850

Horowitz, J.M., Igielnik, R., and Kochhar, R. (2020). *Most Americans say there is too much economic inequality in the U.S., but fewer than half call it a top priority.* Pew Research Center. https://www.pewresearch.org/social-trends/wp-content/uploads/sites/3/2020/01/PSDT_01.09.20_economic-inequailty_FULL.pdf

Jacobs, B.A., and Wright, R. (1999). Stick-up, street culture, and offender motivation. *Criminology, 37*(1), 149–174.

Jacobs, B.A., and Wright, R. (2006). *Street justice: Retaliation in the criminal underworld.* Cambridge University Press.

Jones, R. (1902). Fracture of the base of the fifth metatarsal bone by indirect violence. *Annals of Surgery, 35*(6), 697–700.

Khurshid, A., Ahmad, H., Jaffry, A.A., Khurshid, M., and Ali, G. (2022). A homicide in disguise: How the autopsy dug up clues. *Cureus, 14*(5). https://doi.org/10.7759/cureus.24691

Merton, R.K. (1968). *Social theory and social structure.* Free Press (originally published in 1938).

Messner, S.F., and Rosenfeld, R. (2013). *Crime and the American dream.* Wadsworth (originally published in 1994).

Miller, N.E., Sears, R.R., Mowrer, O.H., Doob, L.W., and Dollard, J. (1941). The frustration-aggression hypothesis. *Psychological Review, 48*(4), 337–342.

Narayan, A., van der Weide, R., Cojocaru, A., Lakner, C., Redaelli, S., Gerszon Mahler, D., et al. (2018). *Fair progress? Economic mobility across generations around the world*. World Bank Group. https://openknowledge. worldbank.org/bitstream/handle/10986/28428/9781464812101.pdf

O'Keefe, D.J., and Medway, F.J. (1997). The application of persuasion research to consultation in school psychology. *Journal of School Psychology, 35*(2), 173–193.

Pew Charitable Trusts. (2012). *Pursuing the American dream: Economic mobility across generations*. https://www.pewtrusts.org/~/media/legacy/uploadedfi les/pcs_assets/2012/pursuingamericandreampdf.pdf

Rios, V.M. (2012). Stealing a bag of potato chips and other crimes of resistance. *Contexts, 11*(1), 48–53.

Romero-Daza, N., Weeks, M., and Singer, M. (2005). Conceptualizing the impact of indirect violence on HIV risk among women involved in street-level prostitution. *Aggression and Violent Behavior, 10*(2), 153–170.

Shukla, K.D., and Wiesner, M. (2015). Direct and indirect violence exposure: Relations to depression for economically disadvantaged ethnic minority mid-adolescents. *Violence and Victims, 30*(1), 120–135. https:// doi.org/10.1891/0886-6708.vv-d-12-00042

Thomas, W.I., and Thomas, D.S. (1928). *The child in America*. Knopf.

Treadwell, J., Ancrum, C., and Kelly, C. (2020). Taxing times: Inter-criminal victimization and drug robbery amongst the English professional criminal milieu. *Deviant Behavior, 41*(1), 57–69. https://doi.org/10.1080/01639 625.2018.1519136

UNODC. (2019, July). *Global study on homicide: 2019*. United Nations. https://www.unodc.org/documents/data-and-analysis/gsh/Booklet1.pdf

U.S. Department of Justice—Federal Bureau of Investigation. (2020). Crime in the United States, 2019. https://ucr.fbi.gov/crime-in-the-u.s/2019/ crime-in-the-u.s.-2019

Vorobej, M. (2008). Structural violence. *Peace Research, 40*(2), 84–98.

Xu, J., Murphy, S.L., Kochanek, K. D., and Arias, E. (2021). Deaths: Final data for 2019. *National Vital Statistics Reports, 70*(8). https://www.cdc.gov/ nchs/data/nvsr/nvsr70/nvsr70-08-508.pdf

2

# Family and Close Relationships

One finding from our exploratory study of reclassified U.S. deaths (see Chapter 1) suggests that the perpetrators and victims in cases of covertly committed murder are disproportionately more likely to have shared a familial or other close relationship compared to those involved in overtly committed incidents. Indeed, an established relationship with a would-be victim—especially if that relationship includes the assumption of trust—would be an advantage for a covert perpetrator. That is because covert violence often requires the perpetrator to have close access to either the intended victim or to an item that they would not hesitate to ingest or have in close proximity. While most people would be suspicious of food or drink that was left on their porch by an unknown person, they would likely put no thought at all into accepting a cup of coffee from a friend or eating a meal prepared by their spouse.

Related to the apparently higher incidence of covert violence within families and friendships is another finding from our study: that women appear to commit covert acts of violence at far higher rates than is reported in official data on violent crime. This may be explained, in part, because of an inverse relationship between women's access to power and their access to family members and friends. The family happens to be the one social institution in which U.S. women are disproportionately deficient relative to men in all three types of power that are relevant to covert violence (that is, physical, economic, and personal). Economically, women in paid work still earn less than men on average (Aragao, 2023), and mothers are more likely than fathers to head a single-parent household (Livingston, 2018). These facts combined help to account for women's higher rate of poverty compared to men (Semega, 2019).

While it may be pure mythology to depict our cave-dwelling masculine ancestors as clubbing their female companions before dragging them off by the hair, the contemporary version of the mythical caveman has its counterpart in reality. It is clear, however, that men's greater-on-average capacity to physically overpower women is exponentially more dangerous when combined with traditional gender roles that legitimate male aggression and encourage female submission, a dynamic that still exists in many American families today. Further, this dynamic illustrates the point at which gendered deficits in physical power intersect with gendered deficits in personal power, lending some explanation for the apparently high rates of covert violence within families and intimate relationships. At the same time, traditional gender roles also tend to provide women with more opportunities for covert violence than men—particularly when their weapon of choice is poison.

Among U.S. households that include a heterosexual couple living together in a committed relationship (whether married or not), most divide domestic duties along traditional gender lines to some extent. This is based on the results of a recent Gallup poll (Brenan, 2020) that investigated which chores are more likely to be shared equally between men and women in the same household, as well as how the rest are divided by gender. While men are much more likely than women to take care of yard work and automotive tasks, women do far more caregiving, cleaning, and meal preparation, including grocery shopping, cooking, and washing dishes (Brenan, 2020). These responsibilities provide women with disproportionate knowledge of household poisons and plentiful opportunities to covertly contaminate the food, drink, or medicine of a family member. Moreover, poison does not require physical strength—or even a perpetrator's presence at the moment of its ingestion—to be employed as an effective weapon of murder. A husband could leave for work carrying a lunch packed by his seemingly loving spouse, only to fall dead halfway through his shift, while the perpetrator remains at a safe distance.

The fact that most of the domestic work frequently performed by women keeps them inside, compared to men's largely outdoor tasks, also may offer additional cover away from the prying eyes of neighbors and their increasingly ubiquitous video surveillance systems. A recent market research survey of U.S. adults (Ferron, 2021) found that, of the nearly 40 percent of households that reported having at least one type of home security product, the most common one was a video camera (or video doorbell), which surpassed in presence even the traditional home security system with professional monitoring. Another report that provided a breakdown of the market share by video camera types showed that surveillance of the *exterior* of homes accounts for about 60 percent of the global market (Grandview Research, 2020), and forecasts suggest large increases in home security spending over the next few years, largely driven by video surveillance products sold in the United States and Canada (Research and Markets, 2020).

## Retaliating against abuse

Something else that often occurs in secret and mostly indoors is intimate partner violence and other forms of domestic abuse. Like covert violence, these acts are also closely related to power and gender roles. Husbands and boyfriends attack their physically weaker romantic partners at alarming rates, committing the vast majority of both serious and fatal acts of intimate partner violence (National Coalition Against Domestic Violence, 2020). Women who are victimized by this abuse frequently endure it not just because of their physical vulnerability but also because of one or more common (and rational) economic and social vulnerabilities that disproportionately affect women relative to men. They might lack adequate financial resources to support themselves and their children, fear that others won't believe or help them, be concerned that the abusive partner might retaliate against friends and family, and/or believe that the abuse might become even worse.

Men also perpetrate all kinds of child abuse, but at similar rates compared to women—or even lower, for some types of abuse. Indeed, recent data from the U.S. Department of Health and Human Services (2021) on parent-perpetrated child maltreatment clearly show that mothers acting alone account for a significantly higher proportion of such incidents (nearly 40 percent) compared to fathers acting alone (about 23 percent), two parents acting together (21 percent), or one or more non-parent adult perpetrators (about 14 percent). What is unknown is how much of this pattern can be attributed to women's disproportionate responsibilities for childcare compared to men, the steady rise in single-parent households (most of which are female-headed) over several decades, or to women taking out their anger on those who are less physically powerful.

For the physically vulnerable, covert violence may be an effective strategy to retaliate against a stronger, more powerful aggressor. After suffering years of abuse, some women have covertly—and successfully—fought back against their much stronger intimate partners. Likewise, neglected and abused children have employed clandestine means to strike back against their more powerful parents, and mistreated older adults have found ways to enact surreptitious revenge against their younger, stronger caregivers.

Psychologist Lenore E.A. Walker introduced the concept of a "battered woman" in the late 1970s and developed it over the next several years into the notion of "battered woman syndrome." Since then, courts in a number of countries, including Australia, Canada, New Zealand, the United Kingdom, and the United States, have accepted an impressively large body of research indicating that people who have suffered longtime abuse—whether physical, emotional, psychological, and/or sexual—may legitimately use (even deadly) force to defend themselves in situations that they know to be exceptionally dangerous, even when the average person would not necessarily define the situation in the same way.

Over time, two important changes in aspects of U.S. law enhanced the legal potency of introducing battered woman syndrome as a legitimate defense in criminal trials. First, women—or anyone else—who live in fear of being attacked by their abusive partners are not necessarily expected to retreat from their shared residence. The law mandates that they take measures to retreat from the immediate vicinity of their attacker, but only in cases where that is feasible. The so-called "castle doctrine," best known as it relates to a homeowner's right in many states to use deadly force against an intruder in their home, also often applies to domestic violence. In other words, no one is required to leave their (legally occupied) own home to avoid being battered by a spouse or cohabitating partner.

The second change relates to the amount of physical force that is deemed legally appropriate to employ against an abuser. The former standard, which allowed only a proportionate amount of force, had been frequently applied to convict a woman who used a weapon to defend herself against her unarmed husband or partner. This standard would also be applied in the case of a fistfight with equally matched participants where one of them suddenly pulls a gun and fires; that response would be regarded as a disproportionate use of force, given the circumstances. However, the key phrase in the fistfight example is "equally matched." When applied to instances of domestic violence, the abuser and the victim of the abuse are rarely even close to equally matched, and the argument fails to consider the (sometimes substantial) difference between romantic partners—especially among heterosexual couples—with respect to physical strength and body size. An abusive man might be substantially larger and stronger than his wife and, in the absence of weapons on either side, could easily overpower her. And after that pattern has played out multiple times before, it's not difficult to understand her desire to even the playing field in the best way she knows how.

When used as a legal defense in U.S. courtrooms today, it is usually known as the "battered person syndrome" (or it is adapted to fit the case at hand, such as "battered child syndrome"), although no variation of the term is included in the *Diagnostic and Statistical Manual of Mental Disorders* (5th ed.), which is commonly known as the *DSM-5* and is considered the standard classification manual used by mental health professionals in the United States (American Psychiatric Association, 2013). As a clinical diagnosis, then, it would most likely be classified as a type of post-traumatic stress disorder (PTSD).

Since the 1990s, an increasing number of U.S. states have allowed juries to consider longtime past abuse as a mitigating circumstance in cases with a defendant who is charged with attacking or killing their abuser. In such cases, the legal standard shifts from what a *reasonable person* would do to what a *reasonable battered person* would do, in recognition of the severe psychological trauma that frequently results from long-term abuse. This distinction takes into account the intimate knowledge longtime victims of abuse acquire over time that enables them to recognize patterns and predict moments of danger that may not be obvious to others. Walker (2012, p. 324) explained this important notion clearly in an article for the *Notre Dame Journal of Law, Ethics & Public Policy*:

> Most state legislatures define "imminent" as being on the brink of or about to happen, rather than "immediate" which is the colloquial use of the term. This difference is critical in battered women self-defense cases because frequently the women are hypervigilant to cues of impending danger and accurately perceive the seriousness of the situation before another person who had not been repeatedly abused might recognize the danger. They may make a preemptive strike before the abuser has actually inflicted much physical damage, anticipating his next moves from what they know from previous experience.

The first case to shine a worldwide spotlight on the battered woman defense began with the 1989 death of Deepak Ahluwalia in the United Kingdom. Deepak and his wife, Kiranjit, had moved to the United Kingdom ten years earlier, shortly after marrying in their home country of India. During the decade-long marriage, Kiranjit apparently suffered horrific abuse that included physical violence, sexual assault, emotional and psychological trauma, and food deprivation. She later described making multiple attempts to run away from the home, as well as seeking help from her family that never came. After a particularly brutal attack one evening, Kiranjit waited for her husband to fall asleep and then poured homemade napalm over his bed and set it on fire, before running out of the house. Deepak survived for ten days with severe burns over 40 percent of his body before finally succumbing to his injuries. Kiranjit was convicted of murder later that year and received a life sentence.

In 1992, however, Kiranjit's conviction was overturned on appeal because her counsel had failed to inform her that she could plead guilty to manslaughter because of diminished responsibility. In addition to the trauma of repeated abuse, Kiranjit was also suffering from severe depression at the time of the attack that should have been revealed to the court. After a mistrial was declared, Kiranjit was released and the prosecution decided not to pursue a second trial. This case not only highlighted the psychological effects of longtime domestic abuse, but also led to changes in related U.K. laws and was used as a legal precedent to overturn the murder convictions of other women in similar circumstances.

As in Kiranjit's case, most of the *known* cases in which a longtime victim of domestic abuse strikes back against their abuser are those that employed overt violence (for example, guns or knives). However, the clear and often substantial power differential that exists in most of these cases would seem to increase the likelihood of an attacker choosing a covert method. After all, when striking back against a more powerful target, secrecy is an advantage, and the clandestine nature of the method makes it more likely to go unnoticed—or to be mistaken for something else. Indeed, there may be far more of these cases than anyone would ever guess.

In most homicide cases, a history of the victim's abuse may serve to reduce criminal charges or as a mitigating circumstance in sentencing, but it does not often totally let a defendant off the legal hook. At the time of 64-year-old Stephen Clayton's death in July 2018, the authorities believed that he suffered a fatal fall down the stairs of his million-dollar lakeside home in affluent Lake Wylie, South Carolina. A little more than a month later, Clayton's 52-year-old wife of five years, Lana Sue Clayton, was arrested when a toxicology report by a private laboratory detected high levels of tetrahydrozoline (a chemical commonly found in eyedrops that works by constricting blood vessels) in her husband's system. What was originally blamed on an accidental fall now became regarded officially as an insidious case of homicide.

Stephen had been ill and suffering from excruciating pain in the three days leading up to his death, and Lana eventually confessed to poisoning his water with eyedrops during that time. Lana, a former nurse for the U.S. Department of Veterans Affairs, claimed that she never meant to kill him, but, instead, only wanted to make him uncomfortable and sick enough to leave her alone. According to her attorneys, who were quoted in a news story about the case (Pereira and Allen, 2020), Stephen had "hit her, kicked her, and choked her" throughout their marriage, and she was fed up and ready to teach him a lesson. This was Stephen's seventh marriage, and Lana's deadly poisoning ensured that it would be his last.

In court, prosecutors dismissed Lana's victimization defense, arguing instead that she intended to kill her husband to inherit his upscale residence, as well as another approximately $1 million in assets. During the grueling three-day period before his death, prosecutors alleged that she had hidden his phone so that he would not be able to call anyone for help. Facing either the death penalty or life without parole if found guilty of murder, Lana accepted a deal that allowed her to plead guilty to voluntary manslaughter. In January 2020, she was sentenced to 25 years behind bars.

## Furtive family factions

Beyond romantic relationships, families include power dynamics that may leave powerless members feeling mistreated, neglected, or denied entitlements that they deserve. To lack power, though, means that lashing out in an overt act of violence typically would not be a viable or wise option; instead, waiting patiently and out of sight while plotting a covert strike would seem to have greater potential for success. Children generally hold the least amount of power in U.S. families, and that remains true to some extent even after they reach adulthood. For example, most people refrain from using the first name of a parent throughout their entire lives, including when speaking *to* them as well as talking *about* them—even after a parent's death. Many adults comply with parental requests long into adulthood and feel obligated to show them respect and gratitude. Although many people are satisfied occupying a less powerful role in their original nuclear family, especially as they begin to establish their own and move into those powerful roles, there are still others who are deeply resentful.

For some, it takes a long time for the bitterness to simmer enough to boil over. In January 2019, the death of 85-year-old Carolyn Foster, of South New Jersey, was officially ruled as occurring from natural causes. Given her age and medical conditions, which included diabetes and heart problems, it initially appeared that she had passed away while watching television in the home she shared with her 63-year-old son, Thomas Foster. The case was closed for more than six months, until a relative came forward accusing Thomas of being involved in his mother's death. The accusation appeared credible enough to lead the Ocean County Medical Examiner's Office to perform an autopsy on Carolyn's body, the results of which led the prosecutor's office to reopen the investigation into her death. The Office subsequently issued a statement that included: "After conducting a thorough investigation, it was determined (July 12) that Carolyn Foster's 63-year-old, live-in son, Thomas Foster, was responsible for her death" (Gambardello, 2019). A medical examiner determined that Carolyn had suffered severe trauma to her ribs and neck. Thomas was arrested the same day and charged with murder.

Other children who are disgruntled and/or live under difficult circumstances and may suffer from serious mental illness strike at a much younger age. In one extraordinary case that occurred in 2019 on the outskirts of Goodfield, Illinois, a nine-year-old boy took the lives of five family members—two adults and three children—by burning down their residence at Timberline Mobile Home Park in the middle of the night. Only Kyle Atwood, the boy who set the fire, and his 27-year-old mother, Katie, escaped alive. Kyle was initially charged with five counts of first-degree murder, two counts of arson, and one count of aggravated arson, but he was subsequently found unfit to stand trial. According to Kyle's mother, he had serious mental health issues and previously had been diagnosed with a form of schizophrenia and bipolar disorder.

Many countries and some U.S. states have established a minimum age for prosecution, recognizing that young children—which the United Nations General Assembly (2019) defines as those under the age of 14—are incapable of appreciating the consequences of their behavior and, therefore, cannot truly form criminal intent. That does not mean, however, that children who intentionally engage in dangerous behavior that may harm others or themselves should face no consequences; indeed, intensive therapy, ongoing counseling, and psychological evaluation are frequently deemed to be appropriate.

Speaking about Kyle's case, juvenile defense attorney Gus Kostopoulos was quoted in a news story (Dumas, 2019) explaining the inappropriateness of charging a child that young with murder: "Nine-year-olds don't know that Santa Claus doesn't exist. They don't know people die and don't come back to life. I don't know if a 9-year-old can form intent to commit murder." Kyle's own actions seem to corroborate that opinion, as his apparent plan of attack—setting fire to his own residence and then going back inside, only to barely escape with his life—indicates a basic lack of understanding. If he had killed five people using a firearm, perhaps there would have been less ambiguity about his alleged homicidal intentions.

Certain teenagers could be characterized as a kind of temporary sociopath, as research indicates that their brains have not yet developed sufficiently to provide them with a mature sense of conscience and empathy. As a result, a 16-year-old who seems to be normal and decent might still commit a heinous criminal act—one they would not dream of committing if they had only managed to make it to the age of 26 without hurting anyone. If just one thing had gone differently in 16-year-old Marie Robards' life, if she had just managed to reach full adulthood without thinking one malevolent thought, then perhaps she would have lived her whole life without murdering anyone.

In February 1993, Marie was a smart and talented high school junior. She had recently relocated 45 minutes away from the Granbury, Texas, home, where she had lived with her mother and stepfather since the age of five, to move into her father's Fort Worth apartment after a falling out related to her stepfather's infidelity. Marie had spent time with her father, Steven, over the years, but only for a day or two at a time, and she didn't feel as close to him as she did to her mother, whom Marie felt had chosen her (unfaithful) husband over her only child. Still, she desperately wanted to return home. Over the next few months, as she tried to adjust to a new school and home life, something occurred to her: if her father were out of the picture, then there would be no other option but to send her back to live with her mother. So, she came up with a plan and quickly set it in motion.

The first step was stealing some barium acetate from her school's chemistry lab, which was easy for the straight-A student to pull off when a teacher's back was turned. Then she picked the night—February 18—and inserted the highly toxic chemical into the refried beans of the Mexican food her father was having for dinner. In less than an hour, Steven began complaining of a stomach ache, which rapidly worsened into intense pain and difficulty breathing. By the time that paramedics arrived, he was already dead. Without any reason to suspect foul play or to test for barium acetate—it, like most poisons, is not included in routine toxicology tests—the county medical examiner attributed Steven's death to a heart attack.

The same night that her father died, Marie returned to her mother's home and her life in Granbury. Her plan had worked, though the covert misdeed evidently haunted her over the ensuing year. One day in January 1994, Marie, now a high school senior, tearfully admitted her crime to a friend during a study session together. The shocked friend refused to "tattle" for weeks, but the personal torment caused by keeping that secret eventually became too much. She went to a school counselor, who then urged her to inform the police of Marie's confession. Investigators found barium acetate in the chemistry classroom that Marie had attended at the time of her father's death. They also discovered that a page for barium acetate was missing from the school's safety manual, which listed safety precautions and toxicity amounts for each chemical kept in the lab.

Several months passed while authorities completed their investigation, which included a long search for a lab in the vicinity that was capable of testing for barium acetate. When results revealed the presence of the poison in blood samples taken during Steven's autopsy—at a level that was 28 times the lethal amount—Fort Worth police officers headed to Austin, where Marie was by then an 18-year-old student in her first year at the University of Texas. Once confronted with the evidence and accusation, she quickly confessed to the killing. When investigators asked if Steven had been mistreating her, she insisted that he had not and explained that her only motivation was to return home and live with her mother (Hollandsworth, 1996).

The trial attracted enormous public interest, partly because cases of patricide are extremely rare, but also because the likeable and attractive teenager hardly looked capable of such a cold-blooded act. Nevertheless, the jury found Marie guilty of first-degree murder in May 1996, and that meant she faced the possibility of spending the rest of her life behind bars. Instead, the jury opted to recommend a 27-year prison sentence. Marie was released on parole in 2003 after serving just seven years—and then promptly changed her name. It is unlikely that she has committed, or would ever commit, another violent crime.

Then there are young adults who seem to understand very well the consequences of their murderous intentions. One afternoon in July 2015 at an upstate New York medical office, 60-year-old chiropractor Mary Yoder, whom her husband described as "the picture of health" (Gilmour, 2018), suddenly became violently ill and, in a matter of hours, died. She had worked with patients all morning and seemed to feel fine until just after finishing her usual protein shake around lunchtime.

Determining that Yoder had been poisoned wasn't difficult, and even the type of poison was identified rather quickly (it was colchicine, a medication commonly used to treat gout but that is highly toxic when misused). What seemed to baffle everyone involved in this case, though, came down to the *who* and the *why*. All the evidence seemed to point to Yoder's young-adult son, Adam, including a vial of colchicine that was found in his car, an order for the drug that used an email address in Adam's name, and an anonymous letter sent to police that directly named him as the culprit. Although mother and son had a good relationship and Adam seemed to have nothing to gain from her death, convictions do not require an established motive. A jury in this case may very well have had enough evidence to convict him of murdering his own mother.

In the end, the real culprit was revealed to be 24-year-old Kaitlyn Conley, who was both Adam's ex-girlfriend and the receptionist at Yoder's chiropractic office. Conley was arrested nearly a year after the poisoning, and her motive was reportedly revenge against Adam for the couple's last breakup (Gilmour, 2018). Conley's first trial for second-degree murder ended with a hung jury in May 2017, but a second jury convicted her of manslaughter. She was sentenced to 23 years in prison in January 2018. Perhaps this case fits better as an example of covert violence in the workplace, but it certainly should have appeared here if things had turned out differently for Adam—a mother poisoned by her young-adult son. Most of all, though, it helps to illustrate the difficulty of successfully (and correctly) solving covert cases like this one in all institutional settings.

Ending a romantic relationship frequently coincides with the redistribution of power between the respective parties, each of whom attempts to gain as much of whatever will help them to "win the breakup" (for example, see Fox, 2016, p. 85). For some, this might mean staying in the formerly shared home, taking over the joint bank account, and/or retaining the most joint property; for others, it might mean securing primary child custody, gaining the loyalty of more mutual friends, and/or avoiding a public shaming on social media. In essence, it's all about leaving the relationship with the "upper hand."

An apt example is the tragic end of the relationship between two high school sweethearts in Queensland, Australia. Despite never being legally married, Louis Mahony and Lainie Coldwell had been a couple for 18 years and shared a three-year-old daughter when tragedy struck in August 2009. That is when 36-year-old Mahony called emergency services to report that Coldwell, also 36, had been in a terrible accident just outside their home. Mahony said that Coldwell must have fallen from a ladder while attempting to remove party lights from a tree on their property and hit her head on the rock-strewn ground below. Coldwell was rushed to the hospital, but succumbed to her injuries two days later, and the coroner officially ruled her death an accident. However, when rumors surfaced about Mahony's apparent infidelity and Coldwell's plans to leave with their daughter, some wondered if the accident scene had been staged, and those suspicions only grew with the revelation of a multimillion-dollar insurance policy on Coldwell's life that benefited Mahony. Authorities reopened the case in 2011 and eventually arrested Mahony, who was convicted of Coldwell's murder in November 2017 and sentenced to life in prison.

## The devious deeds of profiteering partners

Sometimes people covertly target their intimate partners in an effort to gain financially. Poisoning seems to be a particularly appealing method of murder in these cases, for a variety of reasons. One is that spouses and cohabiting partners have a lot of unsupervised access to items that the other person regularly ingests and are susceptible to tampering, such as food, drink, and medication. Another reason is that incidents of poisoning are often difficult to detect, both by the person being targeted and by the authorities after the fact. Many highly toxic substances are naturally tasteless and odorless, while the taste and smell of others can be rather easily masked when inserted into something ingestible. In addition, most poisons are not included in routine toxicology testing, and their effects can closely mimic natural causes of death such as cardiac episodes. When given over a long timeframe, especially with steadily increased amounts, a death can look like a merciful end to a mysterious long-term illness. Even when poisoning is detected or suspected in a death, it may be difficult to connect the act to a perpetrator or impossible to prove.

In June 2012, 46-year-old Urooj Khan was a hard-working, married father of a teenage daughter who operated several dry-cleaning businesses with his wife in Chicago, where he had settled in the late 1980s after emigrating to the United States from India. On a whim one day, he purchased a couple of scratch-off lottery tickets at his local 7-Eleven convenience store, and wound up winning the $1 million grand prize. Opting for the lump sum, he would receive about $425,000 after taxes in a few weeks, and he talked to the news media about his plans to use the money to pay off his home mortgage and expand his business. He unfortunately never got the chance; in fact, he didn't even live long enough to receive the check.

Because there was no evidence of foul play or obvious physical trauma, no autopsy was performed, and Khan's death was officially determined to be from a heart attack caused by hardening of the arteries. His body was buried without embalming, in keeping with Muslim tradition, though a pathologist did take and store blood samples. However, Khan's brother, Imtiaz Khan, had noticed increased tension in the family since the lottery win and felt certain that the death was really a murder. Over the next few months, he pleaded with the medical examiner to test his brother's blood for evidence of poison. In September, testing finally revealed the presence of lethal levels of cyanide.

The medical examiner immediately changed the manner of death to homicide and ordered the body to be exhumed for an autopsy. By then, however, the advanced state of decomposition prohibited any discovery of how the poison might have entered Khan's system. This made it nearly impossible to identify the perpetrator, though most suspicion fell on Khan's wife, who had cooked and served the last meal he had eaten shortly before falling ill (Gorner, 2017). In the end, the widow was awarded the dry-cleaning business and two thirds of the lottery proceeds, and Khan's daughter (from a prior marriage) received some investment properties and the other third of the winnings. The case remains open and has not yet been solved (Gorner, 2017).

The fact that poisonings may resemble—or even trigger—natural deaths would be especially appealing to perpetrators looking for a life insurance payout. Virtually all policies would pay in the event of a death by heart attack or chronic illness, for example, but other manners of death may come with caveats. Some insurance companies won't pay out in the event of a suicide (or a death that looks like one), while others treat homicides and/or accidental deaths differently from natural ones.

In June 1986, 42-year-old Stella Nickell, of Auburn, Washington, phoned emergency personnel in a panic to report that her 52-year-old husband, Bruce, had fallen unconscious after taking Excedrin capsules for a headache. Paramedics rushed Bruce Nickell to the nearest hospital, where he died shortly after arrival. An autopsy was performed, and the cause of death was officially recorded as stemming from emphysema.

Six days later, 40-year-old bank manager Sue Snow collapsed in the bathroom of her Auburn home shortly after taking Excedrin. Paramedics rushed her to the same hospital where Bruce was taken nearly a week earlier, and she also died soon after arriving. Unlike the Nickell autopsy, the pathologist who examined Snow's body noticed the scent of bitter almonds and knew about its association with cyanide poisoning. Further testing confirmed the presence of cyanide, and that warranted another look at Bruce Nickell's cause of death, which also turned out to be from cyanide poisoning. Both bottles of the pain reliever from the separate Nickell and Snow households contained capsules containing cyanide, triggering an area-wide recall of Excedrin products.

Investigators recovered another four bottles of cyanide-laced painkillers in the Auburn area, but not all were Excedrin. In fact, a contaminated bottle of Anacin-3 was found on a shelf at the same grocery store where Stella Nickell purchased the tainted Excedrin, suggesting that the poisonous capsules had not originated with any single company, but were tied to one specific location. Investigators began to consider the possibility that the bottles had been placed on retail shelves by either an employee or a regular customer. It wasn't long until they zeroed in on Stella as the culprit who had distributed the tainted painkillers in pharmacies and grocery stores around the area, apparently in the hopes of creating the impression of a random ambush reminiscent of the 1982 Chicago-area Tylenol poisonings.

In December 1987, Stella Nickell was arrested on multiple federal charges of product tampering, with two resulting in death. Attempts to determine her motivation revealed that she stood to receive an extra $100,000 under the terms of Bruce's otherwise meager life insurance policy if his cause of death was considered an accident (for example, unknowingly ingesting poisoned medication) rather than a result of natural causes (for example, emphysema). Stella's daughter from a previous relationship testified to the FBI that her mother had become profoundly bored with Bruce, that their marriage had become overrun with arguments, excessive drinking, and overwhelming debt, and that she believed Stella had poisoned her stepfather.

Perhaps the most important piece of circumstantial evidence was that all of the tainted capsules also contained tiny flecks of green crystals, which testing revealed to be a substance used in home aquariums to eliminate algae. Not coincidentally, Stella Nickell had a fish tank in her home and used an algae killer with the same active ingredient. Following the instructions to crush the crystals into smaller pieces, Stella apparently mixed that process with her preparations for the cyanide-laced capsules. Moreover, investigators uncovered evidence that she had extensively researched cyanide, including checking out multiple titles on the subject from the local library. The evidence implicating her in the poisonings eventually became insurmountable, and she was found guilty in May 1988 on five counts of product tampering with two resulting in death. She was sentenced to five concurrent prison terms, two for 90 years and three for ten years.

The Khan and Nickell poisonings were one-time episodes that together claimed three innocent lives. Other cases include a heinous series of circumstances in which someone secretly poisons a member of their own family over a period of weeks or months. The perpetrator might even personally consume a nonlethal amount of the poison to enhance the appearance of their total innocence. If the plan goes as expected, the victim's condition will gradually worsen over time until their body finally gives out, creating the impression of a progressive illness. All the while, the faithful spouse wrings their hands with apparent worry and tends to their ailing loved one's every need. When death comes, the easiest conclusion is that the victim succumbed to natural causes or perhaps an accidental overdose.

These are the circumstances surrounding the gradual and excruciating demise of 32-year-old Robert Curley of Wilkes-Barre, Pennsylvania, in

1991. Robert had been experiencing flu-like symptoms for months that steadily became worse. Then came the terrible pain in his hands and feet, and then the severe vomiting. By the time his hair started falling out, he had to be hospitalized. It seemed that every time his condition began to improve, his wife, Joann, would visit and celebrate the progress with pizza, a milkshake, or some other treat. After she left, he tended to take a turn for the worse. One evening, from his bed at Hershey Medical Center, Robert tried to tell a nurse that his wife was attempting to kill him. The next morning, he went into cardiac arrest and died.

After an autopsy revealed the presence of thallium, a highly toxic chemical that has been used in rat poison, police launched an investigation to try to identify its source. Initially, it appeared that Robert had been accidently poisoned at work. He was employed as an electrician at a Wilkes University laboratory that stored thallium, and it was possible that he came into contact with the chemical on multiple occasions. However, when advancements in forensic testing compelled the exhumation of his body for a second autopsy three years later, the results indicated that something much more sinister had occurred.

At the time of his death, Robert Curley had a level of thallium in his system that was 900 times the lethal dose. Moreover, tests proved that the poisoning had occurred over the period of a year, beginning prior to his employment at the Wilkes University lab and ending just hours before he died. It was later learned that Joann had systematically added the poison to her husband's drink containers for about 11 months, beginning shortly after their wedding day. Her final episode of covert violence occurred when she brought a thermos full of her special blend of iced tea—plus a massive dose of thallium—to his hospital bedside the night before he died. Assuming that the authorities would want to test the other family members for evidence of the poison, Joann had even taken a small dose herself and given some to her toddler daughter in an attempt to throw them off the scent.

Joann was finally arrested and charged with first-degree murder in December 1996, more than five years after her husband's death. Prosecutors said that her motive was to collect on a $300,000 life insurance policy, as well as to avoid having to share a $1.7 million civil judgment that she received in damages after her first husband's death in an automobile accident. To avoid facing a possible death sentence, Joann accepted a deal to plead guilty in exchange for a 20-year prison sentence. She served every bit of that time and was released in December 2016 at the age of 53.

Like Joann Curley, a big payout was on Lynn Turner's mind when she killed not just one husband, but two. Turner's covert weapon of choice, however, was ethylene glycol—the active ingredient in antifreeze. Lynn, of suburban Atlanta, had been married to 31-year-old police officer

Glenn Turner for less than three years when he suddenly fell ill with flu-like symptoms and had to be hospitalized in March 1995. One day after being treated and released, Lynn said she found him dead upon arriving home. Glenn's death was officially determined to be natural and due to an irregular heartbeat.

Lynn collected $153,000 from Glenn's pension and life insurance and then moved in with firefighter Randy Thompson, with whom she had been having an affair. Less than six years later, 32-year-old Thompson, with whom Lynn had two children, was found dead under circumstances that were virtually identical to those of Glenn Turner's death. Lynn gained only $36,000 for Thompson's death, however, because his $200,000 life insurance policy apparently had lapsed. Nonetheless, it seemed like more than a coincidence.

It was Glenn Turner's mother who contacted Randy Thompson's mother to express her condolences and share information. The moms convinced investigators to take a closer look at both cases, and testing revealed that both men had died from ethylene glycol poisoning. Investigators thought that Lynn had probably inserted antifreeze into food and/or drink, since the liquid is odorless but has a sweet taste. Lynn was first tried for Glenn's murder and found guilty in 2004, just ten months after Thompson's death. In 2007, she was convicted of murdering Thompson and sentenced to life in prison without the possibility of parole. In August 2010, Lynn was found dead in her prison cell of an apparent suicide; she was 42 years old.

Taking a few pages out of Lynn Turner's playbook—and then adding a few of her own—Stacey Castor, of upstate New York, murdered two husbands with ethylene glycol and then attempted to murder her own daughter while simultaneously framing her for her two spouses' deaths. Stacey married her first husband, Michael Wallace, in 1990, and the couple had two daughters, Ashley and Bree, before 38-year-old Michael died suddenly in January 2000 of an apparent heart attack. Stacey collected $55,000 in life insurance and one year later met the man who would become her next husband, David Castor. They married in 2003, and barely two years later, he was found dead of an apparent suicide. This time, though, an astute detective noticed enough oddities—and similarities—in each death that he decided to dig deeper.

In September 2007, authorities exhumed Michael Wallace's body for an autopsy and found the telltale sign of ethylene glycol poisoning: crystal formations in the organs. When Stacey was brought in for questioning, it became clear that she was the prime suspect. That is when she put a new plan into action. First, while Ashley was at school, Stacey typed a document in her daughter's voice that included a confession to killing both her father and stepfather, as well as an intention to commit suicide. After Ashley returned home, Stacey offered her several alcoholic drinks that were laced with a variety of prescription medications and then put her to bed. Bree discovered her sister unconscious and barely breathing the next morning, and alerted her mother, who had no choice but to call 911. Ashley was rushed to the hospital in the nick of time, survived, and testified against her mother at the subsequent trial. In the end, Stacey was convicted of second-degree murder (for David Castor's death), attempted murder (of Ashley Wallace), and forging David's will. She was sentenced in March 2009 to 51 years in prison, where she died of natural causes in 2016 at the age of 48.

It seems that men who perpetrate covert violence against an intimate partner to gain financially are less likely to use poison, which illustrates the fact that (particularly in heterosexual relationships) men less often than women have a need to overcome physical powerlessness. Instead, men might use surreptitious means to attack a romantic partner because they lack other types of power, such as economic or personal advantage. In fact, male perpetrators in these cases very often compensate by using physical strength to enact their devious plots.

In September 2015, 59-year-old Harold Henthorn was convicted of killing his second wife, Toni (Bertolet) Henthorn, a 50-year-old eye surgeon who fell more than 100 feet to her death three years earlier while hiking in Colorado's Rocky Mountain National Park. The couple were celebrating their 12th wedding anniversary, and the death at first appeared to be a tragic accident. But the fact that Harold was the beneficiary of multiple insurance policies on Toni's life totaling $4.7 million, combined with the unusually damaging fall—Toni had suffered brain hemorrhaging, a fractured neck, and blunt trauma to the chest, abdomen, and pelvis—raised suspicions, which only grew when the authorities were made aware that Harold's first wife, Sandra "Lynn" (Richell) Henthorn, had also died in a freak accident. In May 1995, 37-year-old Lynn was supposedly helping her husband of more than a decade change a flat tire along a Colorado roadside when the jack inexplicably slipped and caused her to be crushed to death under the weight of the car. It was officially ruled an accident, and Harold, her visibly distraught widower, subsequently collected about $500,000 in life insurance. Although the authorities suspect that Harold also murdered Lynn, so far he has only been found guilty of deliberately pushing Toni off the mountain cliff. For that crime he was sentenced to life in federal prison, where he remains today.

Timothy Boczkowski also killed two wives, but he opted to stage fatal accidents inside the home rather than in nature or on a roadside. Like Harold Henthorn, Timothy nearly got away with killing his first wife, Mary Elaine, whom he strangled in the bathtub of their Greensboro, North Carolina, home in November 1990. That death was initially ruled inconclusive and presumed to be an accidental drowning, leaving 36-year-old Timothy free to move to the Pittsburgh, Pennsylvania, area. Shortly after arriving, he married 31-year-old Maryann Fullerton, who died four years later in an apparent drowning in the family's hot tub. However, inconsistencies in his story and unusual bruising on Maryann's body raised suspicions.

After the Pennsylvania medical examiner determined that Maryann had been strangled, the North Carolina authorities took another look at their case and subsequently ruled that Mary Elaine, too, had died from homicidal asphyxiation. Timothy Boczkowski was convicted in 1996 of killing his first wife and sentenced to life in prison in North Carolina. Three years later, he was convicted of his second wife's murder in Pennsylvania and sentenced to death, which was later overturned and replaced with another life sentence. In late 2018, he was granted parole in North Carolina and was then promptly transferred to serve the remainder of his sentence in Pennsylvania.

Some fortune-seeking perpetrators waste very little time enacting a covert attack. Just three days after their April 2005 wedding, 58-year-old Margaret Vandergulik became both a widow and the heir to 60-year-old Patrick Plumbe's $1 million estate. Plumbe's body was found in his burned-out vehicle after apparently striking a tree in Victoria, Australia, and the authorities initially believed it to be a tragic accident. Concerns from family members, however, prompted the authorities to exhume the body for a second autopsy the following year, when the medical examiner identified a fracture on the rear of Plume's skull that was inconsistent with a vehicle crash. Vandergulik was charged with murder soon afterward, with the authorities alleging that she first struck Plumbe on the back of the head, causing him to lose consciousness, and then placed him in the vehicle, directed it toward a tree, and placed a heavy object on the gas pedal in an attempt to stage the scene as an accident. She pleaded guilty to manslaughter in late 2008 and received a nine-year jail sentence.

Even when a covert act of violence is eventually recognized for what it is, this does not necessarily mean that the perpetrator will ever be held accountable. Following the February 2008 death of 47-year-old British millionaire Barry Pring, for example, family members pointed the finger at his much-younger Ukrainian wife, Ganna Ziuzina, accusing her of coveting his fortune. After celebrating their first wedding anniversary at a Kiev, Ukraine, restaurant, the couple were attempting to hail a ride home when Ziuzina returned to the restaurant to purportedly retrieve a lost glove. In her absence, Pring was fatally struck by a car with reportedly stolen license plates that never slowed down or stopped before fleeing the scene (Morris, 2017). The incident was initially ruled an accident, but was reclassified as homicide in 2011, although so far there has not been enough evidence to charge Ziuzina, who now goes by the name Julianna Moore (Aspinall, 2021).

## Frenemies, noxious neighbors, and collateral damage

In June 1976, 30-year-old Martin "Marty" Dillon set out for a day of skeet shooting in northeastern Pennsylvania with his friend Stephen Scher, a 36-year-old doctor, but he tragically never made it home alive. Scher said he discovered Dillon lying on his back with a shotgun blast to his chest shortly after watching him run (in allegedly untied boots) after a porcupine. The authorities concluded that Dillon had tripped on his own shoelaces and shot himself in a tragic accident. Scher appeared devastated when first responders arrived. He sobbed while dramatically flinging the shotgun that killed Dillon against a tree in an apparent attempt to destroy it.

Although officially ruled an accidental death, Dillon's father, Larry, never believed this. His suspicions only grew over the next 18 months, during which time Scher divorced his wife, married Dillon's widow, Patricia—a nurse who worked in Scher's hospital—and moved with her and her two children to North Carolina. Larry sought the advice of family friend Stewart Bennett, a former police officer and current forensic reconstructionist, who concluded that Scher's story made absolutely no sense. In fact, Bennett eventually produced enough evidence to compel an exhumation of Dillon's body for a second autopsy in June 1995, when the manner of death was officially changed to homicide.

In October 1997, Scher was convicted of murdering Dillon, ostensibly because he was having an affair with Patricia and wanted her husband out of the way, and he was sentenced to life in prison without parole. However, this conviction was overturned nearly two years later because an appellate court ruled that enough time had passed between the incident and Scher's arrest to prejudice the jury. This decision was also overturned in 2002, and Scher subsequently was retried in 2008 and again found guilty of murder and sentenced to life in prison. He died in prison of natural causes in 2010 at the age of 70.

Love and money are among the most common motivations for murder (including those committed via both covert and overt means). Dillon's death by the hand of someone he called a friend—but with whom his wife was having an affair—clearly represents the first motive, and the previous section recounts an unsettling number of cases in which spouses and romantic partners have used covert violence in an attempt to gain financially. Many people have friends in their lives who are so close and trusted that they start to seem like full-fledged family members. Most of these like-family friendships are certain to be genuine and loving, but when that is not the case, the results can be very damaging—or even deadly.

Unfortunately for the Norton sisters, of Llano, Texas, their 13-year friendship with Tim Scoggin, a helpful young man who was several decades their junior, was not at all what it seemed. Scoggin moved to Llano in around 1975 and began working as an apprentice mortician, and that is how he came to meet

Catherine "Girlie" Norton, who owned the only flower shop in town. Girlie, who was in her early 60s at the time, lived with her older sister, Cordelia, on the 70-acre Norton family estate as the only surviving members of a once-prominent family that included their mother, father (who made a fortunate in mining), and three additional sisters. Neither sister had ever married, and the mansion had not received a visitor in decades (Cartwright, 1989).

Scoggin was around 20 years old then and appeared to have no discernible past (at least not one that he cared to discuss); no one in town knew where he had moved from, and he seemed to have no family in the area. Still, he was outgoing and well liked, and he most enjoyed the company of the town's older residents, whom he was happy to help with whatever they needed (Cartwright, 1989). He became especially close with Cordelia and Girlie, who grew to trust and rely on him more and more as time went on. Even after Scoggin moved more than two hours away to take a higher-paying mortuary job in San Angelo, he was frequently seen in Llano, either in the company of the Norton sisters or else running errands or completing odd jobs for them, and he always stayed at the mansion during these visits (Cartwright, 1989).

Back in San Angelo, Scoggin had become good friends with two other older people, this time a married couple named Olgie and Leita Nobles, who lived in the trailer park that Scoggin managed and owned a business called Nobles Air Conditioning that sold evaporative coolers (colloquially known as "swamp coolers"). Scoggin often borrowed money from the couple to stay afloat while (it was later revealed) he tried out various financial schemes, including embezzling from the trailer park business, fraudulently applying for bank loans, and cashing forged checks drawn on other people's accounts (Cartwright, 1989). By the beginning of 1988, he had racked up more than $100,000 in debt to the Nobleses—which included payments he owed after convincing Olgie to sell him their business—and the couple were ready to cut him off. Scoggin was about to take drastic measures.

Scoggin first went to Llano to spend time with the Norton sisters, both of whom had developed sudden health problems after his last visit that made even basic chores difficult to manage. Responding to the sisters' calls for his help, Scoggin was happy to oblige and got right to work preparing meals, running errands, and handling their correspondence and doctor's appointments. Still, the sisters only got worse. Girlie was the first to die, on February 19, 1988, at age 75. Cornelia died the next day at age 83. Scoggin arranged to have both bodies cremated and wasted no time inquiring about their wills, which—much to his shock and horror—did not even mention him. Instead, the sisters left their entire estate in a trust that was to be used to maintain the Llano City Cemetery (Cartwright, 1989).

Scoggin was back in San Angelo the following month when Olgie Nobles became suddenly and violently ill with vomiting, diarrhea, and severe stomach cramps, which worsened over the next three days, when Leita Nobles found her husband dead. Leita, too, had been dealing with milder versions of the same symptoms for months by then, but she had previously been diagnosed with ulcers and perhaps assumed that stress had exacerbated her condition. She called Scoggin to help with the funeral arrangements for Olgie, and soon thereafter, her illness worsened to the point that she had to be hospitalized in early May for two weeks. When she was well enough to be released, Scoggin drove her home, but her health deteriorated further and within a week was the worst. Leita was hospitalized again on May 28, and this time, doctors were determined to find an explanation.

Testing finally revealed a massive amount of arsenic in Leita's system—at a level later determined to be at least three times a lethal dose. Although the heavy metal leaves the bloodstream in a matter of days, it remains in detectable amounts in the hair and fingernails, and scientists were able to determine that Leita had first been poisoned more than five months prior to receiving the final, massive dose. As it turned out, the long poisoning process ended up saving her life, as her body built up enough tolerance over time to allow her to survive ingesting the dose that surely would have killed anyone else. This finding led to the exhumation of Olgie's body, which also tested positive for arsenic poisoning. Then the Norton sisters' remains were tested, and arsenic was found in Cordelia's but not Girlie's (prosecutors theorized that Scoggin poisoned the younger sister with strychnine, which is untraceable after cremation). Scoggin was convicted of three counts of murder, attempted murder, forgery, and theft, and is now spending the rest of his life in prison.

The century-old expression that *good fences make good neighbors* still has relevance today and perhaps should be heeded more often. In 1988, the Carr family, of central Florida, were only guilty of trusting a neighbor. Tragically, this cost Peggy Carr her life and left two other family members partially paralyzed. Although the Carr family had several altercations with their next-door neighbors, George Trepal and his wife, Diana Carr (no relation to the neighbors), they had no reason to suspect that they might be behind an unsigned letter they received threatening harm if they did not leave Florida. Not long after that, Peggy Carr began to suffer from an unknown illness with symptoms including nausea, difficulty breathing, and pain in the extremities. Then teenagers Travis and Duane began to show similar symptoms. All three were admitted to the hospital, but by the time doctors confirmed the presence of thallium in their bodies, it was unfortunately too late for Peggy, who died in March 1989. The children spent months in the hospital but eventually recovered, and several other family members tested positive for thallium but did not require hospitalization.

Investigators uncovered the source of the thallium in the Carr home: an 8-pack of 16-ounce glass bottles of Coca-Cola. Of the three bottles that had not been consumed, all tested positive for thallium, as did the empty bottles that hadn't been discarded. The Coca-Cola Company said at the time that it had received no other reports of illness or tainted beverages and believed that the product tampering must have occurred after distribution. After interviewing Trepal, investigators developed suspicions that only grew when they discovered that he had a degree in chemistry and spent time in prison for operating a methamphetamine laboratory in the 1970s. Trepal was arrested in April 1990 and charged with first-degree murder, six counts of attempted first-degree murder, seven counts of poisoning food or water, and tampering with a consumer product. He was found guilty in February 1991 and sentenced to death one month later; he remains on Florida's death row today.

Sometimes a covert plot to kill misses its target entirely. In March 1986, Julie Williams, a 46-year-old employee at the Transamerica Title Insurance company in Tempe, Arizona, took a drink from the break room water cooler—and then collapsed. She died in a hospital two days later, having never regained consciousness. An autopsy determined the cause of death to be cyanide poisoning and ruled it a homicide. Since she collapsed shortly after drinking the water at work, it was assumed to be the source of the poison and was sent for testing. Two other employees had also taken sips from the water cooler that day, but said a bad taste had made them spit it out before swallowing any of it. Sure enough, the state crime lab found a massive amount of sodium cyanide mixed with the water inside the container. Yet, no one could think of anyone who would want to hurt—let alone kill—Williams.

It turned out that Williams worked with someone named Sandra Harry whose husband had recently tried to kill her by placing poison in the bottle of her favorite liquor. When that failed to work, 32-year-old Lewis Allen Harry Jr. apparently decided that it would be better for his wife to be poisoned at work, rather than at home, to prevent suspicion from falling on him. He took Sandra's work ID card to gain access to her office building over the weekend, placed a massive amount of cyanide into the break room water cooler—he wasn't taking any chances of it not working this time—and returned home. The next day was a tragic one for the Williams family. Lewis Harry, an equipment manager at a local community college, was arrested and charged with attempted murder, which was upgraded to murder when Julie Williams died.

In all, Harry was convicted of one count of murder and four counts of attempted murder, which accounted for the three other workers present in the office—his wife and the two workers who sipped the water and spat it out—as well as the prior poisoning of his wife's drink at home. He was sentenced to life in prison plus 105 years, and he would have to serve at least 95 years before becoming eligible for parole. On the day of the sentencing, an *Associated Press* news story (Rawson, 1987) reported that the prosecutor said he thought "the death penalty would have been appropriate" and that the judge called the act "a deliberate, purposeful, and senseless scheme to kill."

Other incidents of covert violence seem to be random, targeting anyone and everyone in an area of the perpetrator's choosing. These acts are typically carried out by people who lack power in all respects—physical, economic, and personal—and their violent deeds are akin to lashing out against society at large. They feel like they have been *unjustly* mistreated on a regular basis by family members, employers, co-workers, peers, and even strangers on the street. And they have had enough. From 1989 to 1991, a series of pipe bomb explosions had the residents of Grand Junction, Colorado, on edge. In total, four bombs were placed seemingly at random around the city; three of them exploded (one was diffused before it could go off) and two people were killed, with another injured. The bombs appeared to be identically constructed (as homemade versions of trip-wire pipe bombs like the one shown in Figure 2.1 that are used in training exercises by the U.S. Army), and officials believed that the same person had made and placed all of them.

In 1993, 29-year-old former cafeteria dishwasher James Genrich was convicted of these crimes, sentenced to life in prison, and won't be eligible for parole until 2083. However, in a recent twist in the case, the forensic

**Figure 2.1:** Image of a trip-wire pipe bomb

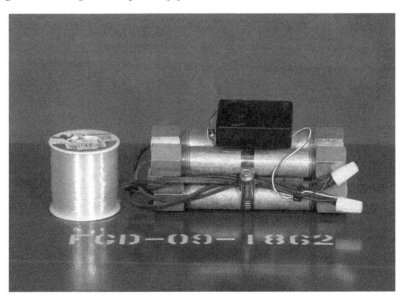

Source: U.S. DOD Defense Visual Information Center/Wikimedia Commons

evidence used to convict Genrich has been called into question, and an appeals court ruled in 2019 that a new evidentiary hearing should be held (see Ashby, 2019). Whether or not it was Genrich who committed the bombings, such covert acts of violence against a neighborhood or city happen from time to time, most likely perpetrated by frustrated, powerless people who are simply not satisfied to get even only with a malicious individual or two, but finally strike back at the entire community.

## References

American Psychiatric Association. (2013). *Diagnostic and statistical manual of mental disorders* (5th ed.). https://doi.org/10.1176/appi.books.9780890425596

Aragao, C. (2023, March 1). Gender pay gap in U.S. hasn't changed much in two decades. Pew Research Center. https://www.pewresearch.org/fact-tank/2023/03/01/gender-pay-gap-facts/

Ashby, C. (2019, August 30). Junction bomber may win new trial. *Daily Sentinel.* https://www.gjsentinel.com/news/western_colorado/junction-bomber-may-win-new-trial/article_8598fca2-cae6-11e9-9153-20677ce05640.html

Aspinall, A. (2021, July 23). "No conspiracy" in Brit husband's hit-and-run death in Ukraine and wife "not part of it." *Daily Mirror.* https://www.mirror.co.uk/news/world-news/no-conspiracy-brit-husbands-hit-24604240

Brenan, M. (2020, January 29). *Women still handle main household tasks in U.S.* Gallup. https://news.gallup.com/poll/283979/women-handle-main-household-tasks.aspx

Cartwright, G. (1989, May). Poisoned with love. *Texas Monthly.* https://www.texasmonthly.com/articles/poisoned-with-love/

Dumas, B. (2019, October 9). 9-year-old charged with first-degree murder for allegedly starting mobile home fire that killed 5. *Blaze Media.* https://www.theblaze.com/news/9-year-old-charged-with-first-degree-murder-for-allegedly-starting-mobile-home-fire-that-killed-5

Ferron, E. (2021, February 10). *2019 Safety.com home security report.* https://www.safety.com/home-security-survey/

Fox, J. (2016). The dark side of social networking sites in romantic relationships. In G. Riva, B.K. Wiederhold, and P. Cipresso (eds.), *The psychology of social networking* (Vol. 1, pp. 78–89). De Gruyter Open Poland. https://doi.org/10.1515/9783110473780-009

Gambardello, J.A. (2019, July 13). S. Jersey woman's death was ruled to be due to natural causes, now her son is charged with murder. *Philadelphia Inquirer.* https://www.inquirer.com/news/son-charged-murder-mothers-death-natural-causes-new-jersey-20190713.html

Gilmour, J. (2018, January 12). He broke up with his girlfriend; she poisoned his mother "to get even," family says. *Fort Worth Star-Telegram*. https://www.star-telegram.com/news/nation-world/national/article194520554.html

Gorner, J. (2017, July 25). Lottery winner's cyanide poisoning death remains unsolved five years later. *Chicago Tribune*. https://www.chicagotribune.com/news/breaking/ct-cyanide-poisoning-death-lottery-winner-met-20170725-story.html

Grandview Research. (2020, May). *Smart home security cameras market size, share & trends analysis report by product (wired, wireless), by application (doorbell camera, indoor camera, outdoor camera), by region, and segment forecasts, 2020–2027*. https://www.grandviewresearch.com/industry-analysis/smart-home-security-camera-market

Hollandsworth, S. (1996, July). Poisoning daddy. *Texas Monthly*. https://www.texasmonthly.com/articles/poisoning-daddy/

Livingston, G. (2018, April 25). The changing profile of unmarried parents. *Pew Research Center*. https://www.pewresearch.org/social-trends/2018/04/25/the-changing-profile-of-unmarried-parents/

Morris, S. (2017, January 24). British millionaire was unlawfully killed in Kiev, coroner rules. *The Guardian*. https://www.theguardian.com/uk-news/2017/jan/24/millionaires-family-claims-he-was-killed-by-ukrainian-bride-barry-pring

National Coalition Against Domestic Violence. (2020). *Domestic violence*. https://assets.speakcdn.com/assets/2497/domestic_violence-2020080709350855.pdf?1596828650457

Pereira I., and Allen, K. (2020, January 16). Woman sentenced to 25 years in prison for poisoning husband's drinking water with eye drops. *ABC News*. https://abcnews.go.com/US/woman-sentenced-25-years-prison-poisoning-husbands-drinking/story?id=68330116

Rawson, W.F. (1987, February 12). Life sentence imposed in water-cooler poisoning. *Associated Press*. https://apnews.com/article/5ce9aaa95af0c969ecd5263d66b1a2cc

Research and Markets. (2020, July). *Home security systems market by home type (independent homes, apartments), security (professionally installed & monitored, do-it-yourself), systems (access control systems), services (security system integration services), region—global forecast 2025*. https://www.marketsandmarkets.com/Market-Reports/home-security-system-market-205573901.html

Semega, J. (2019, September 10). Pay is up. Poverty is down. How women are making strides. U.S. Census Bureau. https://www.census.gov/library/stories/2019/09/payday-poverty-and-women.html

United Nations General Assembly. (2019, July 11). *Global study on children deprived of liberty*. https://undocs.org/en/A/74/136

U.S. Department of Health & Human Services, Administration for Children and Families, Administration on Children, Youth and Families, Children's Bureau. (2021). *Child maltreatment 2019.* https://www.acf.hhs.gov/cb/resea rch-data-technology/statistics-research/child-maltreatment

Walker, L.E.A. (2012). Battered women syndrome and self-defense. *Notre Dame Journal of Law, Ethics & Public Policy, 6*(2), 321–334. http://scholars hip.law.nd.edu/ndjlepp/vol6/iss2/3

3

# Formal Education

On a beautiful Monday afternoon in the late fall of 2008, two men arrived at the Houston, Texas, home of their friend, a philosophy professor at the nearby university. They looked forward to the weekly discussions that focused on the theoretical traditions known as "Continental philosophy" and planned to continue their engaging dialog on Martin Heidegger's *Being and Time* from the week before. A quick glance at their friend's empty carport told the pair that the popular professor must be running late—most likely lingering to entertain the seemingly endless questions of his eager-minded students—but waiting together in the warm Southern sun was no bother. Plus, it wasn't unusual for their friend to be a little late for a meeting now and then; he carried a heavier teaching load than most other faculty members in the department and always prioritized his students' needs above all else.

After more time had passed, the men decided to call their friend's cellphone to check on him. It wasn't until that call went unanswered that they started to worry. Despite the professor's absent vehicle, they thought that he still could be home and mused at how silly they would feel if they had waited outside all that time for no good reason. One of the men tried the front door and found it unlocked. When he tried to push it open, however, something seemed to be in the way. After managing to open the door enough to squeeze by and step inside, the man who had just been chatting and laughing with one friend while waiting for another, who had planned to while away the evening in debate and deliberation, suddenly realized that nothing would ever be the same again. There, at the bottom of the staircase just inside the front door, was the body of his friend—the beloved professor—now with a bluish tint to the skin and blood trickling on the floor behind his head. The man yelled to his waiting companion to dial 911.

The 54-year-old scholar was pronounced dead at the scene. An autopsy revealed the cause to be trauma to the back of the head—presumably from a tumble down the stairs—and the medical examiner ruled it an accidental death. A news release from the Houston Police Department (2008) stated, in part: "Friends found [him] deceased at the bottom of a stairway to his

47

apartment. He had suffered a head injury as a result of falling down the stairs and landing on a tile floor. There were no signs of a struggle." Now 14 years later, this incident officially remains an accident, but that classification is not necessarily permanent. Indeed, it is a good example of an ambiguous death: the immediate cause is clear, but the manner—whether accidental or intentional—is not. This case mirrors numerous others, some of which were initially ruled accidents but later reclassified as homicides.

It is not difficult to imagine either scenario: a trip-and-fall down the stairs or a vicious tumble after a malicious attack. Although unpleasant to ponder, many people are just one misstep away from succumbing to a freak accident— or what looks like one. Consider the case of a 38-year-old Boston University lecturer whose September 2020 death from "traumatic asphyxiation" in a residential elevator stunned all who knew her (and many who didn't). The French instructor, who had also taught at several other Boston-area colleges, was apparently attempting to load an oversized package into the elevator of a residential building when the ill-fated incident occurred. In an *NBC Boston* (2020) news report, the crushing death was described by one building resident in this way: "It was horrifying. It wasn't a cry. I can't even describe what it was. I went out in the hall because I genuinely thought someone was being murdered." Freak accidents like this unfortunately do occur, but how easy is it to tell the difference between such an incident and one that was designed to resemble it?

For that matter, how easy is it to distinguish a naturally occurring heart attack from one that was triggered by an intentional poisoning? Most people would be surprised to know that sudden health emergencies occur with some regularity in the population of U.S. teachers, including numerous cases of *collapsing* deaths in their classrooms that are commonly—whether correctly or not—classified as illness or disease. Moreover, many of those cases involve young-adult and middle-aged educators who previously had few if any serious medical problems. The following examples merely scratch the surface of such incidents:

- During a morning class in September 1997, a popular English teacher at Ellensburg High School in Washington State collapsed and died of an apparent heart attack at the age of 47.
- In April 2010, a 44-year-old biology teacher at Neshannock High School in Pennsylvania collapsed and died in his classroom while tutoring students at lunchtime.
- In January 2011, another 44-year-old Pennsylvania teacher collapsed and died; in this case, it happened while he was giving a final exam in his machine operations class at Pittsburgh Langley High School.
- In October 2012, a 40-year-old science teacher at Menlo Park Academy, an alternative high school in Minneapolis, collapsed and died in her

classroom after saying that she felt faint; her family reportedly had "no immediate clue" as to why she died.

- In September 2013, a 58-year-old special-education teacher collapsed and died of an apparent heart attack while teaching at Modesto High School in California.
- In August 2016, a 43-year-old teacher at Biltmore Elementary School in Jacksonville, Florida, collapsed in her fifth-grade classroom, later dying at a hospital from apparently natural causes.
- In January 2019, a 24-year-old middle school English teacher in Maryland died because of an unspecified "medical emergency" while teaching in her first year at Herbert Hoover Middle School.
- In November 2019, a 38-year-old special-education teacher at Taconic High School in Pittsfield, Massachusetts, collapsed and died after suddenly experiencing "some sort of cardiac event" in his classroom.
- The following month in San Antonio, Texas, a 61-year-old social studies teacher at Southside High School collapsed in his classroom and later died at a local hospital, with no cause of death announced publicly.
- In September 2020, just weeks into the new semester, a fifth-grade teacher in a North Carolina elementary school unexpectedly collapsed and died in her classroom during a staff development day. Officials speculated that the 50-year-old died of "a medical condition."
- In November 2021, a 39-year-old psychology teacher at Topeka High School in Kansas died after he was found unresponsive in his classroom; no cause of death was announced publicly.

## Shifting authority in the classroom

Teachers represent authority figures whose presence in the classroom can encourage or discourage their students' academic successes. They also enjoy some amount of discretion in terms of how they discipline students for various infractions, whether scholastic or behavioral in nature. Until about 50 years ago, teachers' decisions regarding their treatment of students were likely to be accepted outright by both students and parents. On occasion, an objection to one of those decisions might be handled informally between parents and school administrators.

At one time, even the most humiliating punishments for student misbehavior were largely regarded as acceptable. Thus, some teachers responded to inappropriate conduct by having a disobedient student stand in the corner of the classroom and/or wear a dunce cap. Others would strike a student's hand with a ruler or smack their backside with a paddle. To embarrass an offensive student, a teacher may have announced their low grade to the class or forced them to read aloud a note they passed to a friend.

However, in a profound cultural shift, the late 1960s marked the elevation of institutionalized concern for student rights over the preservation of teacher authority. For the first time, expulsions and suspensions of students for "misbehavior" became the basis for lawsuits and court cases in which judges were likely to decide in favor of students rather than teachers or school administrators (Arum, 2003). During the period from 1969 to 1975, in fact, there were more legal challenges to school discipline than in all the previous years combined. This marked the beginning of large-scale change in how discipline was doled out in U.S. schools. For example, public schools in almost every state still employed corporal punishment as of 1976, but many had eliminated this form of discipline altogether by 1990.

Even after the end of corporal punishment in schools, the assumed authority of teachers continued to erode. Many students no longer regarded their teachers' authority as absolute—or legitimate at all—and penalties for student misbehavior were increasingly viewed as unjust and deserving of retribution. Compared to the situation in 1965, when there were virtually no cases of school discipline decided in state and federal appeals courts, by 2007, the number of such cases had escalated to 70 annually (Levin, 2013).

At the very time when more and more responsibilities were being placed on schools for the socialization of youngsters, these court challenges seemed to undermine the school's moral authority with children. Instead, teachers' discretion and decisions were more likely to be questioned, treated with lawsuits, and taken to court. In large part, the lessons in morality and civility that were formerly taught by teachers in their classrooms have shifted to the purview of school psychologists and counselors, resource officers, and courts of law.

## Bullying the teacher

While school discipline eroded after the 1960s, some disgruntled students apparently began to feel entitled to enact a measure of personal justice against any teacher they disliked or felt had wronged them. Students have been known to bully their teachers in a variety of ways. In the classroom setting, a vengeful student might attempt to seize power by causing a disturbance in the class with disruptive conduct and verbally abusive language. Outside of class, a frustrated student might commit an act of vandalism or steal a teacher's personal property. In order to damage a teacher's reputation, a student might file a false report of negligence or incompetence with school administration, members of the school board, or even law enforcement. On occasion, student-on-teacher bullying has been known to escalate into an act of violence. Although official data on student violence against teachers are difficult to find, scholarly studies consistently find that bullying and other forms of nonphysical violence—such as verbal abuse, threats, and intimidation—are far more common than physical attacks (Longobardi et al., 2019). However, given the power dynamics at play, covert violence may be even more attractive to some disgruntled students.

Students generally lack power compared to teachers, and many likely realize that retaliation via overt methods is usually futile. Most elementary and middle school students are smaller in stature than their teachers and therefore lack the ability to lash out with physical force. Yet, even the larger, stronger, and older students would likely realize that threats or the use of overt violence against a teacher would not be generally tolerated by other students and school staff, who greatly outnumber them. Nearly all students lack personal power compared to teachers, who have more autonomy—especially on school grounds—and are more likely to be believed in the event of a teacher–student dispute. And although some students may have more economic power than their teachers, such as those who come from wealthy families and receive generous allowances, this type of power tends to matter less in this context compared to others. Certainly, some high school students have nicer cars and larger spending accounts than many teachers, but that does not improve their grades, reduce the number of rules they must follow, or grant them more freedoms during the school day.

With deficits in the types of power most relevant in this social institution, students with violent intentions toward their teachers are more likely to be successful using covert methods. In contrast, schoolyard bullies usually target students who are smaller, weaker, and/or younger than they are, employing threats and physical violence to intimidate, terrorize, and injure. Bullies have more power than the bullied and, thus, may use overt tactics without fear of serious reprisal. Strikes directed upward in a power hierarchy, however, require careful planning and commission under cover.

Many disgruntled students who strike back via covert violence opt for poison as their weapon of choice. To be clear, relatively few students go to the extreme of seeking revenge against a teacher using a potentially lethal weapon such as poison; most vengeful students employ a far less dangerous method for getting even with an offensive teacher—something more in line with placing a whoopee cushion on the teacher's chair or hiding all the whiteboard markers in their classroom. Moreover, those who do use poison as a weapon are not necessarily bent on causing death and destruction. Rather, these tend to be the deeds of the immature and naïve: juveniles of elementary or middle school age, rather than older teenagers who may be more sophisticated in the ways of the criminal and certainly more capable of understanding the potential consequences of their actions.

Whether or not the full extent of any given incident was realized at the time, there are numerous cases in which vengeful students inserted a harmful substance into their teacher's water bottle, soda can, or coffee cup when it was momentarily unattended. And the reasons for these potentially lethal acts are frequently trivial or practically non-existent (see Figure 3.1). In 1993, a 17-year-old student at a Colorado Springs high school slipped sodium hydroxide, a caustic chemical like that found in drain cleaner, into his teacher's water bottle, apparently in retaliation for the teacher marking an unexcused absence on his official record. When 53-year-old Barbara Lewis took a sip from the bottle, she immediately felt a severe burning sensation in her mouth and throat, and was rushed to the hospital. Doctors fought to save her life as her badly burned throat began to swell to such an extent that she could barely breathe. Fortunately their efforts were successful, but Barbara suffered with medical complications related to the poisoning for the rest of her life.

After a thorough investigation, the student was identified as the probable culprit. Although still a minor at the time of the incident, he was charged as an adult and subsequently convicted of first-degree assault, resulting in an 18-year prison sentence. The following year, however, a judge suspended this sentence and ordered him to serve six years in a juvenile detention center for violent offenders. Shortly after Barbara's death in August 2020 at the age of 79, the local newspaper in Colorado Springs published a story about her life (Earls, 2020) that briefly addressed the incident. Included are remarks from Barbara's daughter, who said that her mother "never looked at herself as a victim" and that she held no ill will toward the student, thinking of him as "just a kid who'd lost his way."

Something similar happened to Susan Ennis in 1994 while she taught in her Littlerock High School classroom in Lancaster, California. When the 32-year-old English teacher drank from her can of Diet Pepsi—which she had placed on the stand that also held the classroom overhead projector and the bottle of fluid used to clean it—she felt a burning sensation in her throat and promptly began vomiting. She was initially hospitalized for six days and again shortly thereafter because of related complications, which will likely never be fully resolved. The 15-year-old culprit was arrested about a week later, after confessing to pouring the cleaning fluid into his teacher's drink can. The student pleaded no contest to a charge of assault with a deadly weapon and was ordered to serve three to five months at a juvenile probation camp, followed by probation until the age of 18, in addition to other penalties that included paying restitution, writing an apology letter, maintaining good grades and school attendance, and staying out of trouble. During the courtroom hearing, the incident was described by the prosecutor as "a very heinous act," by the defense attorney as "a practical joke that went sour," and by the victim as "a senseless act of violence" (Sneiderman, 1994).

Cleaning fluid is frequently used in school-related poisonings, probably because it is readily available and easy to transfer into a victim's drink quickly and covertly. There are quite a few examples of these incidents in

**Figure 3.1:** Reasons students gave for poisoning their teachers

Source: Compiled by the authors from cases discussed in this chapter

just the last decade or two, many of which—thankfully—have not resulted in life-threatening or long-term damage. In 2011, a high school student in Oakland, California, spiked her teacher's coffee with cleaning fluid and bleach. Fortunately, the teacher immediately spat it out and thereby was able to avoid any serious physical injury. Across the country and several years later, in 2017, two middle school students in North Carolina inserted cleaning solution into their seventh-grade science teacher's soda. The victim suddenly became nauseous and developed a headache while teaching his class, and later experienced enough abdominal pain to require hospitalization. He survived, but was quite ill for three days.

These incidents are not confined to American classrooms, of course, and the United Kingdom has not escaped the shock of students who poison their teachers. One such instance appears to have occurred in June 2012, when a 30-year-old teacher at St. Monica's Roman Catholic High School in Prestwich was hospitalized after drinking from his water glass and immediately afterward experiencing a burning sensation in his throat. A chemical analysis of the liquid detected the presence of a cleaning fluid, which was consistent with the whiteboard cleaner that had been found next to the glass on the teacher's desk. Although they did not name any suspects, the authorities suspected that a student in the class had intentionally inserted the cleaning fluid into the teacher's water when he wasn't looking. Once the teacher fell ill, paramedics were called and took him to the hospital, where he was treated for throat pain, breathing difficulty, and pallor.

In some cases, a would-be perpetrator may lose their nerve—or experience a change of heart—and decide to abort the planned poisoning. In 2012, for example, three fifth-graders (two boys and one girl, ages 10–11) in Fresno, California, placed rat poison into their teacher's coffee cup (as well as into the frosting of a cupcake, which the teacher did not consume). The attempted poisoning was foiled when one of the boys apparently got "cold feet" and knocked away the coffee cup just before the teacher took a sip. However, the plot did not come to light until two months later, when the boy's mother bragged to a school administrator that the youngster had saved his teacher's life. The administrator contacted police and had all three children placed in new schools, although it is unclear whether any of them was charged with a crime.

On occasion, a poisoning plot targeting a teacher is foiled by another student. One such instance that occurred in a Warwickshire primary school in England also included another unusual detail: the two ten-year-old perpetrators were apparently part of a group of boys calling themselves "The Mafia" who had written a "hit list" with the names of six teachers they planned to target. One day in May 2015, the boys waited for their 39-year-old teacher to turn her back and then poured bleach in her coffee cup. Fortunately for the teacher, a classmate who saw what the boys did managed to warn her not to drink the tainted coffee before she had the chance to take a sip. The incident—and the hit list—were reported to police, but the boys were suspended from school in lieu of any criminal punishment.

In other cases, perhaps some amount of luck is involved. In 2014, another set of elementary-grade students—this time, two boys ages 9 and 12 in New York City—put rat poison in their teacher's water bottle. After taking a drink, the victim became nauseated and went to her doctor to be checked out, but she otherwise avoided any serious injury and recuperated at home.

Students who target teachers with noxious substances have used a remarkably wide range of materials. In 2015, a high school teacher in New Jersey was rushed to the hospital for emergency treatment after a student had placed Visine eyedrops into her drink at school. The eyedrops contain a chemical called tetrahydrozoline, which reduces redness by restricting blood vessels in the eye, but it can be extremely harmful—even lethal—if ingested.

The New Jersey incident was far from the first time that eyedrops were misused in this way. Nearly ten years earlier, a substitute teacher in Cheyenne, Wyoming, was hospitalized overnight after a 14-year-old student put Visine eyedrops into her cup of coffee. At the time, eyedrops were just starting to become a recognized method of covert attack by young people (a trend that may have been connected to a scene in the popular 2005 film *Wedding Crashers*, which depicts such an act). Indeed, the provider of Wyoming's 24-hour poison hotline reported at least six other cases within two years of the 2007 incident in Cheyenne "in which someone either abused the chemical or provided it surreptitiously to someone else" (Miller, 2007).

Other students have used whatever they happen to have available. In 2000, a San Francisco middle school student was suspended and criminally charged after putting nail polish in her teacher's water bottle; feeling ill, the victim was rushed to an emergency room, where he was treated and subsequently released. At a middle school in Bainbridge Island, Washington, in 2007, two 12-year-olds targeted a teacher whom they knew had a severe strawberry allergy by coating the rim of her coffee cup and water bottle with strawberry lip gloss. The victim was informed of the plot by other students before coming into contact with a dangerous dose of the lip gloss, but she still experienced watery eyes and shortness of breath. In another unusual method of attack, three 12-year-olds at a Florida middle school in 2016 dropped a dangerous amount of red pepper flakes into their teacher's soda can. As the victim suffered from throat and stomach pains that lasted for at least 12 hours, the trio of girls faced criminal charges.

It should be noted that the methods employed by student perpetrators—especially the preteens—may appear to be overt, in that they are sometimes enacted with one or more accomplices and/or in view of other students. For instance, a student who pours cleaning fluid into the teacher's drink during a video presentation while the lights are down would be careful to wait until the teacher's head is turned, but simultaneously might risk being seen by their classmates. And many incidents of teacher poisonings are perpetrated by two or more students operating in tandem, as demonstrated in several of the examples given in this chapter. However, decades of social psychological research have shown that people tend to identify and conform with the expectations of their social group and, thus, are unlikely to blow the whistle on their comrades; this is especially true within the peer groups of adolescents. Moreover, unlike obvious cases of violence committed with firearms and knives, most teachers who have been poisoned were totally unaware of their victimization—until it was too late.

## Discipline and vengeance

The decline in the legitimacy of teacher-administered discipline, combined with shifting ideas about the purpose and efficacy of punishments for bad behavior, has substantially changed the landscape of student conduct policies and procedures in U.S. schools as well as other Western countries. In fact, traditional forms of classroom discipline that effectively managed student conduct in the past now appear more likely to fuel student hostility and resentment. In some cases, the relationship between teacher and student becomes irreparably damaged.

Traditional forms of discipline such as sitting in detention after class, missing part or all of recess, and being reprimanded in front of classmates now tend to enhance a student's feelings of anger and resentment. These methods have also proven mostly ineffective in improving a punished student's classroom behavior, attitude, or academic performance. What they do accomplish, however, is further reducing the small amount of meaningful power that a student may possess during their many years of schooling.

For students in this U.S. social institution, physical power is generally lacking, and economic power is mostly irrelevant, but personal power—an individual's ability to control the manner and direction of their own life, and to be heard, acknowledged, and respected by others—can be gained or lost. Holding some amount of personal power is a fundamental part of being fully human. Yet, traditional methods of punishment strip students of control over their own time, their own bodies, and their own self-expression. They can effectively reduce a student's dignity, reputation, and self-worth. And a sense of powerlessness is at the root of feelings such as anger and resentment, which may intensify over time until eventually erupting into retaliatory violence.

Teacher-initiated measures shown to be more successful in correcting student behavior, in contrast, include verbal or other low-stakes warnings conveyed to a student in private, as well as nonadversarial conferences between teachers and parents. These kinds of methods tend to work because they focus on identifying problems and solutions while maintaining the autonomy and dignity of everyone involved. Even if no clear resolution is achieved, respectful dialogue that recognizes all views and focuses on the future will allow for the collective retention of personal power. More importantly, carefully strategized teacher responses to the unacceptable behavior of their students are unlikely to generate deadly secret plots targeting them (Morrison, 2014).

Unfortunately, school discipline has instead increasingly headed in the direction of so-called "zero tolerance" and the development of student conduct policies that are increasingly punitive and overzealous. They don't allow second chances for rule-breakers or opportunities for reform or restitution—one strike and you're out. Mirroring patterns in the U.S. criminal justice system that have led to mass imprisonment—the United States incarcerates more people per capita than any other country in the world—many offenses in schools now carry mandatory punishments, including in-school or out-of-school suspension, outright expulsion, or contact with law enforcement and the legal system. Advocates for discipline reform in schools argue that zero-tolerance policies are a major force driving the school-to-prison pipeline (Heitzeg, 2009), a term that describes the growing convergence of U.S. schools and legal systems in recent years.

## Nonteacher targets

Despite changes over time, teachers still generally hold a good deal of power in school settings—certainly more than students, but also more than many other staff members—yet they are far from the most powerful group. Administrators, including principals, vice principals, and other managers, are also occasionally targets of covert acts of violence. In 2016, four teenage students in Idaho were arrested after they set a fire at their principal's house that could have killed an entire family. Payette High School Principal Mark Heleker and his wife were asleep in their bed when the boys, ages 14–16, set fire to a trashcan just outside their home. Shortly after the blaze had spread to the house, the couple's adult daughter arrived home late from her job and managed to wake them. Although all three family members (along with their three pets) managed to escape to safety, the house was destroyed.

Although the first boy to be sentenced expressed remorse and insisted that the incident was merely a stupid prank that went awry, social media posts indicated otherwise, including one with a fire emoji alongside the words "burn, bitch, burn" (Moeller, 2017). The authorities suggested that the motive behind the arson was retaliation after one of the boys had gotten in trouble for distributing illegal prescription pills at school that made several students sick. Two of the boys were prosecuted as adults and accepted deals that allowed them to plead guilty to felony second-degree arson, with sentences that included prison time—up to ten years for one and up to 15 years for the other—and payment of more than $30,000 in restitution each. The other two boys were prosecuted as juveniles and pleaded guilty to malicious injury to property and criminal conspiracy; both were sentenced to several years of supervised probation (with the possibility of incarceration for any violations) and ordered to pay the same restitution as the other boys. Heleker retired shortly after the fire and said that he and his wife, a special-education teacher, planned to rebuild their home (Moeller, 2017).

Another example of an incident that would have been much worse without the intervention of someone who happened to be in the right place at the right time occurred in Lorena, Texas. In 2017, a planned attack by two 17-year-old high school students against their vice principal was foiled when a teacher overheard them plotting and managed to warn the administrator. The pair were arrested and charged with making a terroristic threat. According to the arrest warrant, the teenagers were talking about specific details of the plot—"such as poisoning him with an undetectable substance"—and how they planned to "get away with it" (Conlon, 2017). The students apparently became furious with the vice principal after he reprimanded one of the girls for leaving campus during the day in violation of school policy.

It's not just students in educational settings who covertly strike from powerless positions, of course. Early in the 2016/2017 school year, the head custodian at Tavares High School in Florida experienced an immediate burning sensation after drinking from a fast-food soda that she had briefly left unattended. In the time that it took to clean up the cafeteria, someone poured floor-stripper fluid into Jackie Rocket-Smart Hansell's drink, and one gulp left her struggling to breathe. Hansell was rushed to a local hospital for treatment and fortunately survived. Shortly after the incident, authorities arrested custodian Russell Terrance Smith, who reportedly had been quite vocal about his opposition to Hansell's selection for the top janitorial post (Gillespie, 2016).

On occasion, a staff member may call on a student to assist with their covert plot. In April 2019, for example, a school bus driver at a Jamaican community college allegedly offered to pay a student $100,000 to deliver a poisoned cake to a high-ranking administrator who apparently had threatened to fire him. The student refused to take part and alerted the administrator, who then called the police. The case was eventually dismissed when the administrator declined to pursue it after months of legal delays.

In other cases, a powerless staff member might target a student whom they perceive to have more personal power than they do. In a 2015 incident in Perry Township, Ohio, a middle school janitor was convicted of criminal damaging after cutting the brake lines on the vehicle of a 16-year-old high school student. Although police chalked it up to a "personality conflict," the problem between David Patron and the teenager's family ran deeper. Patron had complained numerous times to the school district about the student's alleged "bullying, intimidation, and threats of physical harm" against his daughter, who had a learning disability, with apparently no satisfactory response or resolution (Freeman, 2015). Although Patron undoubtedly planned for the student to have some kind of "accident," the teen instead quickly noticed the car problem upon driving and was unhurt in the incident. Patron's sentence included some jail time—most of which was served under house arrest—as well as community service and monetary restitution.

## What about higher education

Although colleges and universities are also part of the social institution of formal education, covert violence committed by students against professors appears to be exceedingly rare. When such instances do occur, typically they are perpetrated by the youngest students and also tend to resemble the cases more usually seen in high schools. At Sweden's Vasteras College of Design and Construction, several 18-year-old students engaged in at least three separate covert attacks in October 2013. In one episode, several teachers fell ill after drinking coffee that was made and served by a student, two of whom were sick enough to be rushed to the hospital complaining of throat problems immediately after drinking the coffee. In another incident, the police were called after a student fell on a staircase that subsequently was discovered to have been purposely unscrewed. Shortly after that, a student set a fire in the school building. All of the incidents were attributed to the actions of a small group of disgruntled students.

Instead, college students who are angry and want to get even with a professor are more likely to use overt methods than covert ones. In August 2000, a recently dismissed doctoral student in comparative literature at the University of Arkansas, Fayetteville, shot and killed his former faculty adviser and then committed suicide. In an eerily similar incident on the other side of the country and more than a dozen years later, a former graduate student at the University of California, Los Angeles, killed himself shortly after fatally shooting an engineering professor whom the student accused of stealing computer code. Six months after that incident, in December 2016, a University of Southern California doctoral student stabbed to death the psychology professor who led the lab where he was conducting research. These horrific examples of overt murder represent the kind of violence that is more commonly seen in higher education compared to the covert methods in lower-level schools.

This pattern is also clearly explained by examining the workings of power. As full-fledged adults, college students generally have far more power (of all types) compared to students in high school and lower grades, as well as a smaller deficit compared to the power of their professors. In contrast to teachers, professors have less control over student behavior and spend far less time with their students, since most college classes meet only three hours a week spread over two or three days. In addition, most professors have a private office and teach in a variety of different classrooms, which substantially limits their students' physical access to them and their workspaces. This is important because such access is often necessary for covert methods of violence to work. While an unattended coffee mug on the teacher's desk may provide an opportunity for a covert poisoning, a college professor would generally either leave the mug in their locked office (for example, to run to a meeting or the restroom) or remain in sight of it (for example, while lecturing at the front of a classroom). Moreover, college students typically have more recourse than younger students to protest any perceived mistreatment through official channels—for example, they can drop the class of a professor they dislike, file an appeal after receiving a poor grade, and/ or submit a negative course evaluation that could damage their professor's chances for tenure and promotion.

   Thus, the philosophy professor whose death at the bottom of the stairs was described earlier really may have been the victim of a freak accident. If, on the other hand, the incident was an act of covert violence that was designed to *look* like a fatal fall, the likelihood of the perpetrator being one of his students would be quite small. Rather, a relatively powerless colleague, neighbor, friend, or family member would be a much better bet.

## References

Arum, R. (2003). *Judging school discipline: The crisis of moral authority*. Harvard University Press.

Conlon, S. (2017, February 10). Second Lorena High School student arrested in alleged plot to kill administrator. *Waco Tribune-Herald*. https://wacotrib. com/news/police/second-lorena-high-school-student-arrested-in-alleged-plot-to/article_37f19465-efa4-529b-93a7-9a81bf3d8695.html

Earls, S. (2020, August 29). Longtime teacher, community "Grandma," led by example, and with her heart. *The Gazette*. https://gazette.com/news/longtime-teacher-community-grandma-led-by-example-and-with-her-heart/article_73154ca8-e7cc-11ea-b7d5-4fb0e7f30c51.html

Freeman, K. (2015, May 1). Janitor charged, accused of cutting student's brake lines on his car. *Fox 8 Cleveland*. https://fox8.com/news/janitor-charged-accused-of-cutting-students-brake-lines-on-his-car/

Gillespie, R. (2016, September 2). Cops: Promotion to head custodian led to poisoning. *Orlando Sentinel*. https://www.orlandosentinel.com/news/lake/os-tavares-janitor-poisoned-20160902-story.html

Heitzeg, N.A. (2009). Education or incarceration: Zero tolerance policies and the school to prison pipeline. *Forum on Public Policy*. https://files.eric. ed.gov/fulltext/EJ870076.pdf

Houston Police Department. (2008, December 2). *Investigation into man's death at 1915 Windsor #5*. http://houstontx.gov/police/nr/2008/dec/nr120208-3.htm

Levin, J. (2013). *Blurring the boundaries: The declining significance of age*. Routledge.

Longobardi, C., Badenes-Ribera, L., Fabris, M.A., Martinez, A., and McMahon, S.D. (2019). Prevalence of student violence against teachers: A meta-analysis. *Psychology of Violence, 9*(6), 596–610. http://dx.doi.org/10.1037/vio0000202

Miller, J. (2007, December 14). Prank with eye drops could result in criminal charges. *Casper Star Tribune*. https://trib.com/news/state-and-regional/prank-with-eye-drops-could-result-in-criminal-charges/article_8fb40b52-de76-56be-861a-03fd42e7c952.html

Moeller, K. (2017, January 19). Teens plead guilty to setting fire that burned down Payette principal's house. *Idaho Statesman*. https://www.idahostatesman.com/news/local/crime/article127595324.html

Morrison, N. (2014, August 31). The surprising truth about discipline in schools. *Forbes*. https://www.forbes.com/sites/nickmorrison/2014/08/31/the-surprising-truth-about-discipline-in-schools/?sh=629e36883f83

*NBC Boston*. (2020, September 16). A BU French teacher was killed in an elevator accident in Allston: Here's what we know. https://www.nbcboston.com/news/local/a-french-teacher-was-killed-in-an-elevator-accident-in-allston-heres-what-we-know/2195738/

Sneiderman, P. (1994, June 28). Student, 15, is sentenced in poisoning: Courts: The youth pleads no contest to assault charge for putting caustic solution in teacher's soda. *Los Angeles Times*. https://www.latimes.com/archives/la-xpm-1994-06-28-me-9426-story.html

4

# The Workplace

On July 20, 2006, Adrienne Miranda, of Lutherville, Maryland, received the call that every parent dreads. On the line was her ex-husband, with whom she shared two sons, informing her that their 19-year-old son Joseph was dead. The only information known at that time was that the teenager had been found face down in the dirt after somehow being crushed under a Bobcat earth mover while working at his summer landscaping job. Joseph had recently graduated from high school and planned to attend college to become a landscape architect when his life was cut short. In the ensuing days after the tragedy, questions swirled around what exactly had happened to Joseph. One of the two witnesses at the scene—the Bobcat driver—seemed as confused as anyone, while the other told a shifting story about a supposedly freak accident.

What seems clear is that Joseph had been well liked by the other employees and was quickly climbing the workplace ladder, having already achieved a promotion to foreman at the time of his death. However, such success at a young age sometimes breeds resentment from others—especially those with more work experience or years with the company who have been denied the benefits and/or promotions to which they believe they are entitled—who feel the sting of powerlessness.

In any case, Adrienne never believed that her son's death was an accident, even though this was the official ruling of every county authority that reviewed the case, including the prosecutor's office in Carroll County (where the landscaping company was located), the prosecutor's office and police in Baltimore County (where she and her son lived), and even prosecutors in nearby Frederick County. Nevertheless, the grieving mother vowed to fight as long as it would take to prove that her son was murdered—or to at least convince someone in authority to listen. It took more than five years, but she finally succeeded.

In August 2011, Joseph's manner of death was officially changed from accident to homicide. Dr. Zubiullah Ali, the assistant medical examiner for Baltimore County who agreed to re-examine the autopsy report, found "no plausible explanation as to why [Joseph] was in a face down position while run over by the Bobcat" (Hermann, 2011), instead concluding that he had been pushed or knocked down into the path of the reversing machine. Adrienne believed she knew exactly what had happened and appeared to assign no blame to the driver of the earth mover. Rather, she said the other worker who was present at the scene deliberately pushed her son into the Bobcat's path, calling him "a killer [who] is getting away with murder" (Miranda, n.d.). At the time of this writing, however, no formal investigation of Joseph's death has been reopened, despite its reclassification as homicide. The state's attorney for Baltimore County, Scott D. Shellenberger, was quoted in a news story (Hermann, 2011) as saying: "I respectfully disagree with the conclusion now reached by [Dr. Ali] that [Joseph's] death was at the hands of another." Case apparently closed.

Although covert violence in the workplace is perhaps rarer than in other social institutions, the connections to power may be clearer—particularly because power itself tends to be more explicitly distributed there than in other institutions. Most workplaces have overt hierarchies that clearly delineate amounts of financial compensation (that is, economic power), as well as prestige and autonomy (that is, personal power), which have important implications for workers' lives. Disgruntled employees usually lack sufficient clout to retaliate directly against an offensive co-worker or boss without seriously harming themselves. Operating in the open, they risk being demoted, overlooked for a promotion, placed in an inferior company location, or terminated altogether. If, however, they fight back while concealing their identity and using a covert weapon, it is conceivable that a disgruntled worker can achieve the sweet revenge they seek without being harmed or hassled—or even detected at all.

We have become all too familiar with incidents of workplace violence that make a big splash on television news, newspapers, and social media. These tend to be the mass-violence episodes with large body counts in which a disgruntled worker—or *former* worker—decides to get even with the boss and/or their co-workers for alleged mistreatment through the barrel of a high-powered rifle. Almost always a middle-aged white man who either faces imminent termination or has already been fired, the perpetrator in these cases *literally* kills and injures, but often while simultaneously attempting to *figuratively* kill the company or the brand. He knows that the on-the-job rampage will shine a spotlight on the company—leaving it with a black mark or perhaps bankrupt after settling lawsuits filed by victims' families—as well as generate widespread anxiety among supervisors and bosses everywhere (Fox and Levin, 1994). Given the overt violence of these instances, many of these perpetrators consider their rampage as the beginning of the end; indeed, most are dead by the end of it and often by their own hand.

In sharp contrast, some acts of company covert crime are so well planned and executed that it is never absolutely clear whether they were intentionally committed at all. Even when all other possibilities have been ruled out, there may still be a lingering doubt as to the cause of the company disaster. Was it an accident? The work of a disgruntled customer? Just a hoax? This is frequently the appeal of covert crime from the viewpoint of the criminal, as the impetus for the deviant act may never be discovered and, thus, the identity of the perpetrator may remain forever hidden. Of course, a resentful employee doesn't need to injure or kill someone to get even with a company; covert violence has many layers and many possible outcomes.

## Killing the company

Because of the average employee's enormous power deficit relative to their employer, covert violence offers a rare opportunity for powerless perpetrators to strike a blow against a mighty company. Although innocent strangers may be harmed or killed in the process, the attacker would likely consider them to be merely collateral damage that will ultimately strengthen the impact of the strike. Product tampering, in particular, has proven to be an effective method used by disgruntled workers seeking to surreptitiously retaliate against their employer.

During the 1990s, news reports that syringes were being discovered inside bottles and cans of Pepsi swept North America. Although most of those reports turned out to be false, the first certainly occurred. In 1990, a clerk at a Steinberg grocery store in eastern Ontario noticed a syringe in an unopened Pepsi bottle and removed it from the shelf. After investigating the incident, Canadian officials concluded that the likely culprit was a disgruntled employee of the bottler, EastCan Beverages of Ottawa. Four years later, syringes and other dangerous objects were allegedly found in Pepsi cans by unsuspecting U.S. customers in what turned out to be a rash of publicity-seeking pranksters.

The perpetrator of the confirmed case likely intended no particular harm to the unsuspecting customer who would encounter the syringe; rather, the ultimate harm was meant for the PepsiCo company itself. Because of the worker's huge power deficit compared to PepsiCo, this form of covert violence would have offered a rare opportunity for the powerless employee to strike a blow against the mighty company. Although that perpetrator was never identified, the motive seems quite clear: to reduce the bottom line and damage the reputation of their employer.

Three years after the Canadian incident, it appeared that the perpetrator had struck again, this time in the United States. On June 9, 1993, a couple from Tacoma, Washington, reported that they were looking in an empty can of Diet Pepsi for a prize-winning word to complete the phrase "Be young, have fun, drink Pepsi," but instead found a syringe. Retired salesman Earl "Tex" Triplett, 82, and his 78-year-old wife Mary, said they didn't notice the needle when pouring the drink into a glass the night before, but were certain there was no plausible way that it could have been inserted after the can was opened, as they did not use hypodermic needles or have contact with anyone who did. Although the authenticity of this incident has been questioned throughout the years, it seems more likely than not that it did happen just as the Tripletts described. As in the prior case, the most likely explanation again is that the tampering was done by someone employed at PepsiCo. Also like the prior case, the perpetrator likely never intended to harm the customer who would encounter the foreign object in their drink; rather, the ultimate damage was meant for PepsiCo.

What is certain in what came to be known as "the Pepsi syringe crisis of 1993" is that the majority—if not all—of the subsequent reports of found items in Pepsi cans that came flooding in from across the United States were bogus. After the Tripletts turned over materials to the local health department, their story was picked up by local news media. Then the larger, regional media came calling. Then the national media. By June 14, just five days after the Tripletts' initial report, nearly a dozen more consumers—some as far from the West Coast as Ohio and Louisiana—had claimed that they, too, had found a syringe in a can of Pepsi. More reports came over the next several days, eventually reaching over 50 claims of foreign objects found in Pepsi cans in at least 23 states (*Associated Press*, 1993). Although syringes were the most common items reported, other dangerous objects that consumers claimed to find in Pepsi cans included a bullet, wooden screws, a vial of crack cocaine, a sewing needle, and a hunk of dark-colored goo.

The reports were officially declared a hoax on June 18, only nine days after the Tripletts' discovery, and very few trickled in thereafter. That was especially good news for PepsiCo's crisis-management team, which was working overtime to quell the rumors and restore public trust. The company distributed a series of video news releases to hundreds of local TV stations across the country that were seen by 187 million viewers (Sennewald and Christman, 2008). Based on a combination of the apparently effective public relations campaign, the short duration of the hoax, and the typically short public memory, PepsiCo suffered minimal losses and Diet Pepsi sales quickly rebounded.

Many of the hoaxsters, who mostly inserted the foreign objects into their own cans, were arrested for making false claims. Most said they did it hoping to make a quick buck, gain some media attention, or both. After arresting one of the tricksters—a man from St. Petersburg, Florida, who claimed to find screws in his can of Diet Pepsi—a police officer was quoted in a news story (*Associated Press*, 1993) recounting the man's explanation for his crime: "He said, 'I didn't do it for the money. It was for attention. I just wanted somebody to pay attention to me.'"

Although most of the reports about items found in Pepsi cans were false, at least one—but more likely two—definitely did happen. Unfortunately, misdeeds by production-line workers are not all that unusual, and they pose an ongoing threat to public health and safety. In 2014, Gregory Stanton, a 44-year-old contract worker at a Kellogg cereal factory in Memphis, Tennessee, filmed himself urinating into a bucket and then dumping the contents onto the Raisin Bran production line. The malicious incident went unnoticed for two years and was only discovered because Stanton posted the video online in 2016. After being identified, he was arrested and—facing a possible three years in federal prison—decided to accept a deal and pleaded guilty to tampering with consumer products in 2018. In May 2019, he was sentenced to ten months in prison and ordered to pay $10,000 in restitution. What is perhaps most disturbing about this incident is that he might never have been apprehended if he hadn't decided that internet publicity was worth the risk to his personal freedom.

Stanton's apparent motive was to punish the company for its executives' actions related to an intense labor dispute with the full-time workers' union. At the time, the Kellogg company had ordered the lockout of more than 200 employees at the Memphis factory who were members of the Bakery, Confectionery, Tobacco Workers and Grain Millers labor union, which cut off their pay, health insurance, and other benefits. The dispute stemmed from the union's rejection of company proposals to reduce wages and hire more part-time workers. The lockout dragged on for ten months, finally ending on the order of a federal judge who sided with the union.

It seems that U.S. workers' rights are violated more frequently than many people realize. Human Rights Watch (2019) released a report revealing widespread workplace abuses in U.S. chicken, hog, and cattle slaughtering and processing plants, noting "alarmingly high rates of serious injury and chronic illness among workers." This includes an average of eight worker deaths per year from 2013 to 2017 because of an at-work incident. The report also cites evidence of harsh working conditions, including long shifts without breaks and unreasonably high production quotas that "can limit workers' access to adequate sanitation facilities." In addition, the report notes that the U.S. Occupational Safety and Health Administration (OSHA) "has raised concerns about the accuracy of data on occupational injuries and illnesses in the industry, as well as incentives that may exist to limit reporting," which surely indicates that such violations are far more prevalent than official data suggest. Although retaliatory behavior that endangers the health and/or safety of the public is far from excusable, it's not difficult to imagine how suffering such indignities could manifest in abhorrent behavior.

Other cases have resulted in the loss of consumers' lives. An infamous example is the 1982 crisis that came to be known as the "Chicago Tylenol Murders." In the span of only a few days—from September 29 to October

1—seven Chicago-area residents died after ingesting Extra-Strength Tylenol capsules that had been laced with a lethal dose of potassium cyanide. The first victim was 12-year-old Mary Kellerman, a seventh-grader from suburban Elk Grove Village whose parents gave her one Extra-Strength Tylenol capsule after she woke up with a sore throat and runny nose. Soon after ingesting it, she collapsed and died. The following day, two more people died after ingesting Extra-Strength Tylenol: Illinois Bell employee Mary McFarland, 31, of Elmhurst, and 27-year-old Mary "Lynn" Reiner, of Winfield, who had recently given birth to her fourth child with her husband Ed.

Then, police found the body of United Airlines flight attendant Paula Prince, 35, in her Old Town apartment after she had missed a scheduled dinner with her sister and then failed to report to work the next day. She too, had died of cyanide poisoning after taking Extra-Strength Tylenol that she had just purchased from a Chicago Walgreens drugstore, which later identified her on a surveillance recording and released the still frame shown in Figure 4.1. By October 1, three members of the Janus family— 27-year-old postal worker Adam, his 25-year-old brother, Stanley, and Stanley's 19-year-old wife, Theresa—had all died from cyanide poisoning after ingesting Extra-Strength Tylenol from the same bottle. At this point, police officers began riding through Chicago neighborhoods warning local

**Figure 4.1:** Surveillance image related to the infamous 1982 Tylenol poisonings in Chicago

Source: Boston Magazine/Wikimedia Commons

residents over a public address system about the potential danger of taking Extra-Strength Tylenol.

Late on October 1, Chicago Mayor Jane Byrne held a press conference and announced that all bottles of Tylenol would be immediately pulled from Chicago store shelves. Officials assumed that some unknown deranged person was responsible for placing the cyanide-laced Tylenol bottles on the shelves of various supermarkets and drugstores in and around Chicago. In addition to the five contaminated Tylenol bottles that were linked to the seven deaths, three others were discovered in retail outlets in the area—and none elsewhere.

On October 4, the Chicago City Council passed an ordinance requiring all over-the-counter drugs to be sold in tamper-resistant packaging. The next day, Johnson & Johnson, the company that manufactures the popular over-the-counter pain reliever, issued a recall of all Tylenol products nationwide. On October 6, New York City resident James William Lewis sent a letter to Johnson & Johnson in which he took credit for the deaths and demanded a $1 million payout to make him stop. Evidence linking Lewis to the poisonings was totally absent, and he later was sent to prison after being convicted of extortion. Looking back at the crisis 30 years later, Richard Brzeczek, then-superintendent of the Chicago Police Department, was quoted in *Chicago Magazine* (2012) as saying: "It wasn't James Lewis. James Lewis was an asshole, an opportunist. He tried to extort some money from Johnson & Johnson, and he went to jail."

In 1983, the passage of the so-called "Tylenol bill" made tampering with consumer products a federal offense in the United States. However, it wasn't long before the crisis appeared to resurface—this time in the vicinity of New York City. On February 8, 1986, 23-year-old Diane Elsroth of Peekskill died after ingesting cyanide-laced Tylenol in Yonkers. All sales of Tylenol capsules had been banned throughout the state just two days later, and soon after that, Johnson & Johnson announced that it would no longer manufacture Tylenol or any other over-the-counter drugs in capsule form. Greater protections were granted in 1989, when the U.S. Federal Drug Administration mandated *tamper-proof* packaging for over-the-counter drugs.

Most, if not all, of the incidents after the confirmed Chicago-area poisonings were likely copycats. Still, no one was ever charged with the original covertly committed murders. Credible evidence suggests that the most plausible perpetrator was a disgruntled employee at Johnson & Johnson. The most compelling reason for this was that, even though the tainted Tylenol bottles were purchased from different retail outlets and did not share the same lot number, all came from the same distribution center on their way to drugstores and grocers in the Chicago area.

This view was most publicly touted by Scott Bartz (2012), a pharmaceutical industry insider and former Johnson & Johnson employee whose self-published book accused the company of disregarding the possibility of a revenge motive in order to avoid liability for the multiple deaths. Bartz also alleged that the Tylenol capsules that killed Mary Reiner came from the hospital where she gave birth days before her death; if true, the typical security surrounding such a venue would seem to make the risk of theft or tampering extremely remote.

The Tylenol brand was rescued with the advent of caplets, which—unlike the easy-to-open capsules before them—were solid pills that were difficult to alter, but still had a gelatin coating for easy swallowing. In less than a year, sales rebounded to prior levels and the Tylenol brand continued to be favored among over-the-counter pain relievers. Moreover, Johnson & Johnson received much praise for its response to the mass poisonings at the time, and the case study continues to be used as an exemplar of crisis communication in college textbooks and classrooms across the United States.

In some cases, product tampering has been used by disgruntled workers as a means of exacting revenge against a co-worker or supervisor. By lethally contaminating a popular consumer product, the perpetrator hopes to lay the blame on their associate and make them appear negligent or incompetent. In January 2003, a Family Fare Supermarket near Grand Rapids, Michigan, recalled 1,700 pounds of ground beef after dozens of customers became sick with nicotine poisoning after eating meat purchased at the store.

The poisoning was intentional and exemplifies how interpersonal conflict, especially between people with different amounts of power, can result in actions that threaten the wellbeing of innocent bystanders. After a recent argument with his supervisor, 39-year-old Family Fare employee Randy Jay Bertram mixed an insecticide containing a high concentration of nicotine into 250 pounds of ground beef. In an apparent effort to get his supervisor in trouble, Bertram poured the poison into 1–3 pound packages of the meat while they were being prepared for sale and then watched as they were picked up by customers. The vengeful worker was arrested soon after the poisonings, pleaded guilty, and was sentenced to nine years in prison. It was fortunate that none of Bertram's victims died or suffered long-term or permanent illness.

## Revenge of the "pissed-off" workers

Although repulsive—as well as seemingly juvenile—secretly urinating in beverage containers is a fairly common tactic employed by disgruntled workers seeking to get back at co-workers and/or bosses for what they see as unfair treatment. In March 2018, Conrrado Cruz Perez, a 47-year-old baker at a Vadnais Heights, Minnesota, restaurant, was charged with two misdemeanor counts of adulterating a substance with bodily fluids after he urinated into the water bottle of a co-worker who had rejected his romantic advances. The woman testified that she noticed the taste of urine in her bottle about 15 times over a period of a few months. On June 4, Cruz Perez accepted a deal that allowed him to plead guilty to just one of the counts in exchange for serving one year on probation and complying with pre-sentencing mental health recommendations.

Another case that occurred over several months targeted the entire coffee-drinking staff in one Akron, Ohio, workplace. During the spring and early summer of 2005, 49-year-old postal worker Thomas Shaheen poured urine into the break room coffee pot and then watched as his co-workers drank the adulterated brew. Shaheen, a 13-year veteran of the U.S. Postal Service, was apparently jealous that other employees had been given work privileges denied to him. He was eventually caught when suspicious co-workers set up a camera in the break room and obtained video evidence of Shaheen tainting the coffee with urine on two occasions in July. Shaheen was fired from his job and later pleaded guilty to two misdemeanor charges of tainting food. He was sentenced to six months in a jail work-release program and ordered to reimburse his former co-workers for the expenses they incurred to make the secret recording. At sentencing, he apologized and was quoted in a news report (*Associated Press*, 2006) as saying: "I don't know what became of me. I hope you find it in your hearts someday to forgive me."

Something similar happened a few years later, this time at a water treatment plant in Culpepper, Virginia. In March 2009, 49-year-old James Carroll Butler directed his anger toward co-worker Michael Utz by pouring urine from a toilet into the pot of coffee that Utz was brewing for the staff. Before anyone drank any of the tainted coffee, Utz noticed a foul odor emanating from the pot and notified a supervisor. The concoction was then sent to a lab for testing, which revealed the presence of both urine and fecal matter.

Although it is possible that Butler was trying to frame Utz by making it look like he—the one brewing the coffee—had committed the disgusting deed, Butler eventually confessed. He was fired from his job and convicted of a criminal misdemeanor, for which he was sentenced to one year in jail with 11 months suspended. At the sentencing, he expressed regret and was quoted in a news story (Moran, 2014) as saying: "I am very much ashamed of my stupid and childlike behavior." After one month's jail time, Butler later found himself back in court—this time on a civil matter—to answer a lawsuit filed by Utz, who was seeking $728,000 in damages. In April 2014, a jury awarded Utz just $1 in compensation, but an additional $5,000 in punitive damages.

It's interesting that those who commit covert acts like tainting food and drink with urine or other vile-but-not-often-deadly substances tend to express feelings of remorse and shame more often than perpetrators who use more lethal substances. Further, these "pissed-off" perpetrators rarely complain publicly about their sentences or refer to their misdeeds as jokes or pranks. These tendencies are likely connected to the juvenile quality of these acts—and the fact that they are so, well, *gross*. Like other covert acts of violence, this type is enacted by powerless people seeking to gain some amount of personal satisfaction by demonstrating, even if only to themselves, that they can outwit their more powerful target. However, by selecting such a childish and disgusting method, they raise the stakes of being caught, for the result would be a far larger deficit to the perpetrator's supply of personal power than if they had used a method more likely to evoke feelings of fear, shock, or horror (rather than revulsion).

Consider the case of German toolmaker "Klaus O." (German privacy laws prohibit the release of his last name), who worked at a metal fittings company in Schloss Holte-Stukenbrock for nearly 40 years and, according to police, may have been responsible for a string of worker deaths over that time (Romo, 2019). Although so far there is no proof that Klaus had any involvement—or even that any of the 21 deceased former employees was, in fact, murdered—the 57-year-old was arrested in May 2018 and charged with trying to kill his co-worker. The victim had complained to management after noticing a white powdery substance on his sandwich for the second day in a row. They decided to install a hidden camera in the employee break room, and the resulting footage clearly showed Klaus secretly tampering with the lunches of multiple co-workers. Analysis of the white powder found on the complainant's sandwich revealed it to be lead acetate, a highly toxic substance capable of causing serious organ damage or immediate death if ingested. Klaus, who never expressed remorse or offered an explanation for the poisonings, was convicted of attempted murder in March 2019 and sentenced to life in prison.

Examining the likely power shifts subsequent to two different acts of covert contamination in the workplace—putting urine in the office coffee pot versus poisoning a colleague's food with a toxic heavy metal—helps to illustrate the inherent risks and rewards of each type. One possible outcome is that either perpetrator avoids capture, in which case they could gain personal power in the form of self-satisfaction for accomplishing their goal. Unlike the perpetrator who used urine, the perpetrator in the poisoning scenario might also stand to gain economic power (for example, if the target becomes unable to work and their more senior job becomes available).

The other possible outcome, of course, is that either perpetrator gets caught, in which case both would lose economic power when they are fired from their job, but only the perpetrator who used urine would face a substantial loss of personal power—likely dropping to even lower levels than before the misdeed. Their use of a bodily fluid as a weapon against others would be seen as something less than human, or at least beneath an adult human being. The perpetrator who used a toxic heavy metal, on the other hand, would lose *some* personal power—mostly related to the resulting conviction and sentencing—but they also would likely gain personal power in another sense. For some, this power is gained from the demonstration of advanced knowledge (of chemistry, in this case) and/or extraordinary stealth; for others, it's derived from the infamy of having done something so extraordinarily terrible.

Within U.S. culture—as well as others in which competition and individual achievement are highly valued—crimes that appear to be especially clever, complex, or clandestine appear to fascinate members of the public and garner media attention similar to that of celebrities and other public figures. Although members of the public generally do not condone these crimes, their comments frequently suggest admiration of the effort, skill, patience, dedication, and/or intelligence that it took to carry them out. Some crimes may be described as "brazen," "bold," or "daring," and some perpetrators as "gutsy," "having a lot of nerve," or "going to great lengths." Yet, these words and phrases are also frequently used to describe extraordinarily good deeds. This creates a fuzzy distinction between *very good* behaviors and *very bad* behaviors, while simultaneously placing clear value on the *very*.

## References

*Associated Press*. (1993, June 18). Pepsi tampering arrests grow. https://apnews.com/article/0cb2a89a2d5390d08b7a15530c56d747

*Associated Press*. (2006, September 19). Man sentenced for putting urine in coffee. *The Pantagraph*. https://www.pantagraph.com/news/man-sentenced-for-putting-urine-in-coffee/article_aa2d8075-3cd5-58e9-9b83-82020b8c82e1.html

Bartz, S. (2012). *The Tylenol mafia: Marketing, murder, and Johnson & Johnson*. New Light Publishing.

*Chicago Magazine*. (2012, September 21). Revisiting Chicago's Tylenol murders. https://www.chicagomag.com/Chicago-Magazine/October-2012/Chicago-Tylenol-Murders-An-Oral-History/

Fox, J.A., and Levin, J. (1994). Firing back: The growing threat of workplace homicide. *Annals of the American Academy of Political and Social Science, 536*(1), 16–30.

Hermann, P. (2011, October 15). Five years later, death ruled accident now a homicide. *Baltimore Sun*. https://www.baltimoresun.com/news/crime/bs-md-co-miranda-homicide-family-20111008-story.html

Human Rights Watch. (2019, September 4). *"When we're dead and buried, our bones will keep hurting": Workers' rights under threat in US meat and poultry plants*. https://www.hrw.org/report/2019/09/04/when-were-dead-and-buried-our-bones-will-keep-hurting/workers-rights-under-threat

Miranda, A. (n.d.). About the author. *Stand up for Justice*. http://www.thescentofmyson.com/

Moran, L. (2014, April 11). Virginia worker who peed in colleague's coffee pot coughs up $5,001 in damages. *New York Daily News.* https://www.nydailynews.com/news/crime/man-peed-co-worker-coffee-coughs-5g-damages-article-1.1753296

Romo, V. (2019, March 9). German man who poisoned co-workers sentenced to life in prison. *NPR.* https://www.npr.org/2019/03/08/701617766/german-man-who-poisoned-coworkers-sentenced-to-life-in-prison

Sennewald, C.A., and Christman, J.H. (2008). *Retail crime, security, and loss prevention: An encyclopedic reference.* Butterworth-Heinemann.

5

# Politics and Government

Covert violence has always played an important role in supplementing conventional warfare. In 2016, for example, British special forces waged covert military operations in Yemen, Syria, Iraq, and Libya (Curtis and Kennard, 2019). However, two days after the U.K. Secretary of State for Defence stated that there were no plans to deploy troops to the Middle East, reports surfaced that British troops had secretly blown up an Islamic State vehicle carrying large amounts of explosives. Clandestine attacks by weaker operatives have also occurred, with devastating consequences in the United States, a country widely known for its military might. The most infamous examples include the December 1941 bombing of Pearl Harbor by Japanese forces and the September 11, 2001 attacks perpetrated by al-Qaeda terrorists; each resulted in the loss of thousands of American lives, many more injuries, and massive destruction of property.

Moreover, biological warfare has a centuries-long history around the world, as well as in the United States, such as the British colonists' deliberate distribution of smallpox-infected blankets to Native Americans in the 1760s (Frischknecht, 2003). In modern U.S. history, the worst bio-terrorism attack— in terms of number of victims—occurred nearly 40 years ago in Oregon under highly unusual circumstances. In the early 1980s, several hundred followers of the Bhagwan Shree Rajneesh, the Indian spiritual leader who founded the Rajneesh movement, established a compound in northern Oregon, about an hour east of Portland. The Rajneeshees, as the followers were known, unnerved the residents of nearby Antelope (which has maintained a population under 100 since the 1940 Census). At first, it was because they all wore the same red clothing, participated in communal chanting and meditation, and demonstrated other odd forms of behavior. Later, it was because they began to outnumber the longtime residents and take over local politics. In fact, the city of Antelope was briefly renamed Rajneesh, Oregon, around this time.

When the Rajneeshees decided to aim even higher politically, they set their sights on the county seat of the city of The Dalles. The outnumbered group tried various strategies to sway the 1984 county election in their favor, including bussing in thousands of homeless people from around the United States who promised to vote for the Rajneeshee candidates—until that move was blocked by an emergency rule for suspected voter fraud. Another strategy was to ensure low voter turnout among the local residents, who were likely to oppose the group's candidates. After rejecting an idea to poison the local water supply, they decided to sicken the population another way: by contaminating the salad bars at multiple restaurants and other public areas in The Dalles with salmonella.

A total of 751 people became ill, many severely but—incredibly— none fatally. The scheme failed to win any real political influence for the Rajneeshees and marked the beginning of the end for the group's stay at the U.S. compound. In the end, the group's leaders were prosecuted for the mass poisonings, as well as other federal and state crimes, including attempted murder, wiretapping, and arson. The Bhagwan Shree Rajneesh was given a suspended sentence, paid $400,000 in fines, and was deported to India, while three of his deputies served prison time before also being deported.

## Nations at war

In a typical combat situation, warring nations act to achieve the upper hand over their enemy on the battlefield using conventional weapons such as rifles, machine guns, grenades, and the like. On occasion, however, a combatant seeking to reduce its vulnerability might violate the international rules of warfare in covert and/or clandestine ways, which may prove highly effective. Covert operations are those that aim to conceal the source of an attack or the identity of an attacker, while clandestine operations disguise the attack itself. In either case, an enemy force strikes with the element of surprise to even the playing field or gain the upper hand against a more powerful opponent. If all goes as planned, they will then slink back into the shadows undetected—via secrecy or obfuscation—while leaving a trail of mass anxiety, casualties, and destruction in their wake.

The threat of biological weaponry of mass destruction was realized well ahead of time. By 1900, there already existed two international declarations— in 1874 in Brussels and in 1899 in The Hague—prohibiting the use of poisoned weapons, as well as several additional treaties in subsequent years. Perhaps the threat was so apparent by 1900 because biological weapons had already been used on a smaller scale for centuries. Between 1155 and 1863, documented attacks between political rivals included: contaminating water wells with dead bodies, selling wine mixed with the blood of leprosy patients, launching projectiles coated with the saliva of rabid dogs, and distributing blankets and clothing used by smallpox and yellow fever patients. By 1675, there was even an agreement in place between Germany and France not to use "poison bullets" (Frischknecht, 2003).

Unfortunately, none of the established declarations, treaties, or agreements included provisions for oversight and control or repercussions for violators. Thus, by the early 20th century, government entities began to quietly investigate the possibility of using biological toxins and infectious agents on a large scale against their enemies. During the First World War (July 1914 to November 1918), the German army was the first to implement mass biological warfare (Frischknecht, 2003), though it was still mostly experimental and unleashed on a small scale compared to its use in subsequent wars. Their main strategy was to infect the animals—especially horses—in enemy countries with anthrax and glanders (a bacterial disease mostly affecting horses, donkeys, and mules that is both contagious and highly lethal to humans), either through direct infection or by contaminating supplies of animal feed.

The consequences of Germany's clandestine experiments with bio-terrorism were not lost on members of the global community. In 1925, a treaty known as the Geneva Protocol was signed that prohibited the use of chemical and biological weapons in international armed conflicts. Once again, however, the protocol failed to include any method for verifying compliance. The agreement also did not stop some nations from retaliating in kind or surreptitiously causing disease epidemics against their enemies (Baxter and Buergenthal, 1970).

During the Second World War (September 1939 to September 1945), the Japanese military secretly contaminated more than 1,000 water wells in Chinese villages with cholera and typhus, as well as widely dispersed plague-infested fleas in China's cities and rice fields. In 1940 and 1941, massive numbers of insects were dropped with devastating consequences from low-flying planes onto crops, enemy combatants, and civilian populations in Chinese cities, including Ningbo and Chengde, Hunan Province. In addition, Japanese forces poisoned the food supplies of civilian populations of China by covertly distributing plague-infested dumplings and vegetables. Large-scale bubonic plague epidemics dragged on for years after the war's end, killing an estimated 200,000–500,000 Chinese men, women, and children. It was later revealed that Japan had planned to spread the plague among the population of San Diego, California, during the summer of 1945 (Kristof, 1995), in what turned out to be the final months of the war. However, the Japanese forces surrendered before they were able to implement their undercover plan for the United States.

Japan was not the only nation to resort to unconventional warfare during the Second World War. Shortly after the United States entered the war, Adolf Hitler ordered an extensive campaign of sabotage against the American people and their efforts to support U.S. forces fighting overseas (Dobbs, 2004). In 1942, eight German saboteurs secretly entered the United States with the objective of destroying bridges, railroads, waterworks, canals, and plants that manufactured tanks and airplanes. In what was planned as a two-year operation, the Nazis sought to infiltrate the United States with teams of fifth columnists every six weeks (Dobbs, 2004). The first eight Germans to arrive clandestinely had all spent considerable time living in the United States before the Second World War and spoke fluent English, which gave them a decided advantage with respect to remaining indistinguishable from Americans.

Arriving in a boat from a German submarine in the dark of night on June 13, 1942, a four-man team of saboteurs reached the coast off Amagansett, Long Island, where they attempted to bury their explosives in the sand, but were spotted by the U.S. Coast Guard patrolling the beach. Fearful of captivity after the bungled landing, one of the saboteurs decided to desert his co-conspirators and turn himself in to the FBI, which initiated a large-scale manhunt for the others, who had escaped to New York City. Four days later, a second four-man team landed at Ponte Vedra Beach, just outside of Jacksonville, Florida. They buried their explosives and uniforms near the beach, then walked to Highway 1 and caught a Greyhound bus for Jacksonville, where they blended into the crowd. However, with the assistance of their German informants, U.S. federal investigators apprehended the entire Long Island team on July 22 and the Florida team five days later—before any of the saboteurs was able to cause damage. None of the infrastructure targets was struck, and no other sabotage attempts were made by German forces on U.S. soil (FBI, n.d.).

The saboteurs had been guaranteed by Hitler's regime that they would be paid large sums of money, be exempt from military service, and receive elite jobs after the "Fatherland" won the war. Instead, the ending was not a happy one for the Germans. Six of the eight Nazi saboteurs were executed by the United States for spying. The remaining two, who assisted the U.S. authorities in the manhunt for the others, were imprisoned, but were later freed by President Harry S. Truman. Both were deported to Germany at the end of the war and were generally treated like traitors and pariahs by their fellow Germans. In some cases, they were forced to flee angry crowds that threatened vigilante justice (Dobbs, 2004).

Any combatant might conceivably decide to employ clandestine weapons and/or to strike surreptitiously. Yet, a warring nation with a large power deficit—perhaps after suffering crippling blows, depleting needed resources, or losing an important ally—but that is still desperate to win might be especially likely to resort to the secret use of illegitimate weaponry, including biochemical alternatives, infiltration tactics, and vicious attacks on civilian populations, national infrastructure, and enemy troops. The elements of surprise and camouflage can become tremendously advantageous when situations become dire or otherwise unconventional between warring forces.

At the end of 1944, sensing that its army was on the verge of collapse, Nazi Germany initiated a final attempt to defeat the Allied forces in

Western Europe and drive its enemy to the negotiating table. In what came to be known as the Battle of the Bulge, German forces set in motion an enormous surprise offensive through the Ardennes region of Belgium—a battle that lasted four weeks and engaged a quarter of a million German soldiers against only 80,000 Allies. As illustrated by the map shown in Figure 5.1, the Germans attacked a thinly defended area of the Allied line (the figurative "bulge") that was held in large part by depleted U.S. forces. As a result, an estimated 20,000 American soldiers were killed and another 40,000 wounded. In addition, nearly 4,000 Belgian civilians were killed by German rockets.

Led by Lieutenant Colonel Otto Skorzeny, 22 English-speaking German commandos wearing American uniforms and riding American jeeps and Panzer tanks altered to look like Shermans infiltrated Allied combatants behind enemy lines. Their objective was to collect information, create confusion, and commit acts of sabotage. Although clever as an alternative strategy, Hitler's Americanized offensive failed to stop the superior yet outnumbered Allied forces. Instead, it only hastened the end of the Second World War's European theater and the demise of the Third Reich (History.com editors, 2009). Largely because of the extraordinary efforts of U.S. troops, the Battle of the Bulge is still considered to be "arguably the greatest battle in American military history" (Kiner, 2020).

The Allied victory at the close of the Second World War was certainly not the last time that American forces have been involved in international conflict. After the Korean War (June 1950 to July 1953), the next lasted nearly 20 years. Ignited in November 1955, the Vietnam War (known in Vietnam as the "American War") was fought between the North and South, but with heavy U.S. involvement, finally ending in April 1975 with the fall of Saigon. The Viet Cong—also known as the National Liberation Front of Southern Vietnam—was a guerrilla movement that, along with the North Vietnamese military, opposed the South Vietnamese army and its allies. The superior military strength of the American forces was effectively mitigated by Viet Cong tactics that were as ingenious as they were unorthodox and cruel.

Viet Cong saboteurs, who were poorly equipped to attack conventionally, were instead very effective in rigging booby traps and imposing unobtrusive obstacles to hinder the unchallenged functioning of enemy forces. For example, guerrillas were known to smear feces onto the tips of sharpened bamboo branches known as "punji sticks" and then thrust them into injured enemy soldiers in order to cause serious infections. The Viet Cong frequently employed well-trained swimmer saboteurs—expert divers— who sank, destroyed, or damaged large numbers of U.S. and allied vessels, as well as South Vietnamese bridges and wharves. Their unanticipated

**Figure 5.1:** Map depicting the Battle of the Bulge in the Second World War

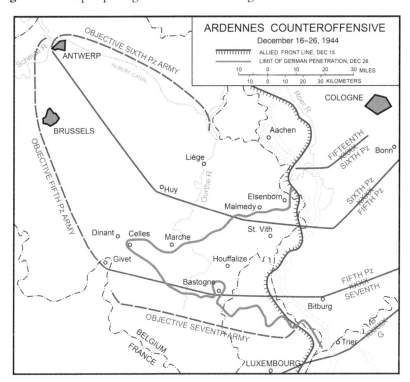

Source: Hohum/Wikimedia Commons

underwater attacks also threatened merchant ships as they unloaded at South Vietnamese ports.

Trained in North Vietnam, the Viet Cong swimmers were able to assemble and deploy land mines, command-detonated mines, and water mines. Despite cold water temperature, strong currents, a rough ocean, and the difficulty of navigating in the dark, they remained in the water for long periods of time, typically equipped with a snorkel, an explosive device, grenades, a signal flare, and a nylon line. In the face of vastly superior American firepower, swimmer saboteurs became an amazingly effective fighting force in support of North Vietnam. Ultimately their guerilla presence may have made the difference between winning and losing the war (Record, 2005).

## Waging war from within

Clandestine forms of violence have been employed with varying degrees of effectiveness by elements of society against their domestic opponents. In August 2020, Russian President Vladimir Putin's most prominent opponent, 44-year-old Alexei Navalny, was poisoned while on a flight to

Moscow from Siberia where he had been campaigning against Putin's party in a local election. At first, Navalny only felt ill, but then he collapsed to the floor and lost consciousness. Suspecting that his disabled passenger was suffering from a drug overdose, the pilot made an emergency landing in the Siberian city of Omsk, where Navalny was rushed to a local hospital for treatment and protective isolation. Forty-eight hours later, as the source of the poisoning became more difficult to identify, Navalny was permitted to leave his hospital bed and fly to a treatment center in Berlin, where physicians almost immediately suspected that he had been poisoned with the powerful military-grade nerve agent known as Novichok. Thanks to the competent intervention of these German medical specialists, Navalny survived.

At first, there was plenty of suspicion but no direct evidence to incriminate Putin or his intelligence services in connection with Navalny's poisoning. Still, the dangerous substance that impaired Putin's opponent was apparently only available to the political upper crust of Russian society. Moreover, this was not the first time that the Russian autocracy had been implicated in threatening Navalny's life. Later, however, Navalny released a video that purported to show a member of Putin's intelligence corps admitting complicity in the poisoning episode. Upon his return to Russia, Navalny was taken into custody and given a two-and-a-half-year prison sentence for violating parole in a 2014 case that he claimed was politically motivated. Many thousands of his angry followers protested on his behalf in cities around the country, and more than 1,000 were arrested (Roth, 2021).

In February 2021, as the United States was preparing to impose sanctions on Russia for Navalny's poisoning and imprisonment, news broke that the Central Intelligence Agency (CIA) had assembled a task force to investigate suspected microwave attacks on approximately 40 U.S. intelligence officers that occurred over several years in Russia, Cuba, China, and possibly elsewhere (Atwood, 2021). The invisible attacks directed microwave radiation at victims that caused traumatic brain injuries and excruciating symptoms that in many cases were difficult to diagnose and/or treat. One former senior intelligence officer was quoted in a *CNN* story (Atwood, 2021) describing his experience in December 2017: "I woke up in the middle of the night with an incredible case of vertigo. The room was spinning. I wanted to throw up. I've been in places like Iraq and Afghanistan; I've been shot at. But this is by far the most terrifying experience of my life." The CIA investigation is ongoing, and no perpetrator had been identified at the time of writing.

In Chile, it took 20 years to officially recognize the murder of a former president, whose death initially was attributed to natural causes. Eduardo Frei Montalva, who led the South American nation from 1964 to 1970, died in January 1982 while hospitalized in a Santiago clinic following a routine operation. When authorities determined that the 71-year-old died from a surgery-related infection, his body was buried and the case was closed.

Yet, some political supporters suspected that Frei had been assassinated, as in recent years he had become an outspoken opponent of the dictatorial regime led by Augusto Pinochet, whose power was increasingly threatened throughout the 1980s (the military dictatorship finally fell in March 1990). The investigation into Frei's death was reopened in 2002, and further analysis of his exhumed remains revealed the presence of "toxic substances" (Vergara, 2019), indicating that Frei had died by poisoning. In January 2019, six men—Frei's personal driver, a former security agent, and four doctors—were convicted for their roles in the murder that occurred nearly four decades earlier. Each conspirator received a prison sentence ranging from three to ten years.

Authoritarian regimes are not alone in their affinity for poisoning the enemy from within. The difficulty of tracing a poisonous substance back to its source has not been lost on members of marginal groups, both large and small, or on so-called "lone wolves" who otherwise lack the material resources to elude responsibility for acts of violence against mainstream government officials and other public officials. Certain violent acts of terror have never been solved, in large part because of an extremist fringe group's use of a hard-to-detect substance capable of causing death to unsuspecting victims. When conventional methods for legitimately confronting a powerful authority figure or mainstream institution are unavailable to a fringe organization, its members might turn to acts of domestic terrorism. Indeed, most acts of terrorism are homegrown and not committed by international operatives (Levin, 2006).

Many acts of domestic political violence have certainly been overtly committed. In a recent example, the U.S. Justice Department arrested almost 200 rioters, extremists, and terrorists on January 6, 2021, who stormed the United States Capitol in support of then-President Donald Trump's stand against the victory of Joe Biden. In all, five people, including a Capitol police officer, died in the siege.

Long before the Capitol attack, the United States had already experienced plenty of incidents of extremist mass violence on its own soil. One series of assaults began just one week after the September 11, 2001 terrorist attacks on the World Trade Center and the Pentagon, in which 2,977 people lost their lives in New York City, Washington, D.C., and outside Shanksville, Pennsylvania. In the second deadly act of terror that received far less attention than the 9/11 atrocity, seven letters containing anthrax spores, in powder form, were mailed from Trenton, New Jersey, to Democratic Senators Tom Daschle and Patrick Leahy and five media offices in New York, Florida, and Washington D.C. After inhaling the poisonous white powder, five people lost their lives, including two U.S. Postal Service employees; 17 others were infected but survived, and 35,000 were given preventive doses of antibiotics. Several contaminated post office facilities and federal office buildings were vacated, emergency rooms were inundated, and the postal system was almost totally disabled. Following the attack, numerous anthrax hoaxes were reported at office buildings around the country (Levin, 2006).

Several different explanations for the anthrax attacks were posited over the years. Coming so soon after the 9/11 attacks, many people originally believed that the poisonings had been initiated by a foreign terrorist group, possibly al-Qaeda, as the second phase of a two-pronged assault on America. This explanation quickly lost credibility, however, when it became clear that the targets of the poisoned letters were exclusively left-wing political leaders and liberal-leaning news outlets. Most observers, including the FBI, thus came to suspect that right-wing domestic terrorists who held a grudge against the left-leaning press and liberal forces in the federal government were responsible. If Osama bin Laden had selected the victims, so the thinking went, he would more likely have targeted right-wing politicians and/or conservative media outlets that supported U.S. participation in Middle Eastern conflicts and whose agenda was more explicitly focused on defeating radical Islamic terrorists.

Soon, however, the possible complicity of a right-wing terrorist group as a viable explanation for the anthrax attacks also lost credibility. The authorities eventually became convinced that manufacturing the finely granulated form of anthrax powder employed in the attacks would have required advanced scientific expertise and that the perpetrator likely possessed an advanced degree in microbiology and had worked in some kind of scientific program within the U.S. government (Willman, 2011). Biological weapons specialist Dr. Steven Hatfill soon became a leading suspect.

During the early years of the FBI's lengthy investigation, Hatfill's residence was raided on several occasions by the federal investigators, his phone was tapped, and he was terminated from his job as a biological weapons scientist. Indeed, he remained under extensive surveillance for more than two years. When the investigation finally concluded in March 2008, Hatfill was cleared of all charges, but his reputation and career had been irreparably damaged by then. In a civil action, he reportedly received a $5.8 million settlement against federal prosecutors.

After wasting years investigating Hatfill, the FBI then turned its attention to another viable suspect, Dr. Bruce Ivins, a well-known scientist who for 18 years had conducted anthrax research at the U.S. government's biological weapons laboratory at Fort Detrick in Frederick, Maryland. According to one widely accepted explanation, Ivins had become anxious that his supervisors regarded his ongoing anthrax inquiry as less than essential and were planning to end the research program. Before it was too late, so the speculation went, he sent the contaminated letters to ensure that anthrax remained an important topic of government research (Willman, 2011).

Investigators ultimately were able to genetically connect the mailed anthrax to a supply kept in a vial in Ivins's lab. The problem, though, was that hundreds of people besides the suspect had access to the lab. Visitors from other institutions and employees at labs in other states had been given anthrax samples from the same vial—in all, about 100 people had worked with anthrax from that source. Moreover, federal investigators never placed Ivins in proximity to the mailbox in Princeton, New Jersey, where the anthrax letters were mailed, and they were unable to locate any anthrax spores in his house, in his car, or on his clothing. Finally, specialists in the area of germ warfare argued that Ivins lacked the expertise required to turn anthrax into an inhalable powder. Ivins was never formally charged for the anthrax attacks, although he remains a chief suspect in the minds of many observers. In 2008, at the age of 62, Ivins took his own life by means of an acetaminophen overdose.

In the aftermath of the FBI investigation of domestic scientists Hatfill and Ivins, there were some observers who proposed a conspiratorial explanation for the anthrax poisonings. This one connected the 9/11 attacks to the subsequent anthrax letters and suggested that the source of both acts was not foreign terrorists, but, instead, individuals operating within the federal government (MacQueen, 2014). Once again, however, that conspiracy theory—albeit a compelling effort to link two horrific terrorist attacks on American soil—has failed to persuade most investigators and members of the public.

On occasion, what may appear to be an intentional act of covert poisoning may actually be no more than a terrible mistake. Accidents do happen, of course, even under the supervision of trained government scientists. In April 1979, spores of anthrax were unintentionally released from a Soviet weapons facility near the city of Sverdlovsk, Russia (now Yekaterinburg). Approximately 100 people lost their lives in the incident. For 13 years, the Russian government refused to accept responsibility for the deadly poison's release, claiming instead that the deaths were a result of contaminated meat. The accidental release was finally acknowledged in 1992 with an official admission by President Boris Yeltsin (Zhang, 2016).

## Extremists and explosives

For various reasons, explosives are the most frequently employed weapons of mass destruction in the arsenal of terrorist organizations (Levin, 2006). Most importantly, terrorists are not always selective in their choice of victims, more often seeking instead to maximize body counts. Shootings or stabbings might efficiently take the life of one or several victims, but guns and knives are usually unsuitable for committing murder indiscriminately by the dozens or hundreds. Poisoning might work effectively as a clandestine method of assassination, yet it still has limited value for fringe groups that seek both to commit mass murder and to terrify survivors and onlookers.

An important exception is provided by the March 1995 coordinated sarin gas attacks on three lines of the Tokyo Metro during rush hour. Twelve passengers were killed, 50 were severely injured, and almost 1,000 others suffered temporary vision problems. Planned and directed by cult leader Shoko Asahara, the deadly attack turned out to be perpetrated by members of the doomsday cult movement known as Aum Shinrikyo. In Aum Shinrikyo's compound, the Japanese police discovered an advanced chemical weapons laboratory capable of producing thousands of kilograms a year of the poison used in the Tokyo subway onslaught. Asahara eventually was arrested for the sarin gas attacks and sentenced to death; he was executed by hanging in July 2018.

Another advantage to using murderous explosives for terrorists is that the source is often difficult to identify. Unlike weapons that leave telltale clues at the crime scene, bombs literally blow away much of the evidence linking them to the perpetrator(s). Few, if any, fingerprints will be found. DNA evidence is unlikely, and there are no bullets or shell casings for ballistic analysis. The devastation done to victims' bodies often means that there are no autopsies to perform. At the same time, explosives may not erase the vivid memories of survivors at the crime scene or protect the terrorists from being identified by eyewitnesses or surveillance footage.

Near the finish line of the 2013 Boston Marathon, two Chechen-American brothers detonated two pressure cooker bombs, killing three people and injuring hundreds more, including 17 who lost limbs. Three days later, the FBI released video images of the suspects. Thanks to a detailed description of the brothers by a severely injured survivor, investigators were able to quickly identify the killers on the recordings from cameras lining the race route and circulate their images.

Explosives have also been known to leave behind a trail of crucial evidence. This was true in the 1995 bombing of the Alfred Murrah Federal Building in Oklahoma City, when right-wing terrorist Timothy McVeigh and his associate sought revenge against the federal government for the 1993 Waco siege that ended in the deaths of 86 people. Although officials originally believed that the deadly Oklahoma City bombing had been the work of foreign extremists, it was later determined that the terrorists were homegrown white supremacists (Levin, 2006).

On the morning of April 19, McVeigh sought to precipitate a revolution against what he regarded as a tyrannical federal government. He and his associate Terry Nichols packed an explosive device consisting of 5,000 pounds of ammonium nitrate and nitromethane on the back of a rented Ryder truck, which they drove to the front of the Murrah Federal Building as it opened for the day. A little after 9 a.m., their bomb destroyed the northern half of the building, as shown in Figure 5.2, taking the lives of 168 men, women, and children, and injuring another 684.

The explosives also destroyed most of the truck, with the important exception of the vehicle identification number on a rear axle that survived the blast. By discovering that number in the wreckage, investigators were able to determine that the truck had been rented from a Ryder agency in Junction City, Kansas. FBI artists created a sketch of the renter based on the recollections of employees who were on duty when he picked up the truck. As investigators canvassed the area with the sketch, the manager of the local Dreamland Motel identified the individual as Timothy McVeigh.

McVeigh was arrested shortly after the bombing of the federal building and charged with a number of offenses that included the use of a weapon of mass destruction. In 1997, he was found guilty on all counts and sentenced to death. His accomplice, Terry Nichols, was sentenced to life imprisonment without the possibility of parole. On June 11, 2001, at the Federal Correctional Complex in Terre Haute, Indiana, McVeigh was executed by lethal injection.

**Figure 5.2:** Image depicting the aftermath of the 1995 Oklahoma City bombing

Source: Leonard Brakebill, Oklahoma Air National Guard/Wikimedia Commons

One of the major problems confronting terrorists who employ explosives as a weapon of mass destruction is securing the necessary equipment without raising suspicion. In some cases, this stage of the covert plot provides an opening for undercover FBI agents to play a surreptitious role themselves— as apparent members of the terrorist team. In June 2006, seven men ages 21–32 were charged with concocting a plot to blow up Chicago's Sears Tower and the FBI headquarters in Miami to "kill all the devils we can" (Shane and Zarate, 2006). Five of the suspects were U.S. citizens, and the other two were Haitian immigrants, one of whom was illegally residing in the United States.

According to FBI agents, their plot was only in "the talking stage," but aimed to organize an Islamic army to wage a jihad in America. After learning of the conspiracy, an unidentified FBI informant posing as an al-Qaeda operative repeatedly met with the ringleader of the group and gathered incriminating information. The final act of the seven conspirators before their arrest was to give the FBI informant a list of equipment they needed, including uniforms, binoculars, machine guns, radios, vehicles, bulletproof vests, and $50,000 in cash. They also provided the informant with their shoe sizes so that he could buy them military boots (Shane and Zarate, 2006).

Some domestic terrorists operate as so-called "lone wolves." An infamous example of covert political violence committed by a single individual is the bombing offensive committed by Theodore Kaczynski, also known as the Unabomber. Not only was the Harvard-educated mathematician alone when he perpetrated his 17-year killing spree, but he was also a loner who despised high-tech society and opted to communicate his message of destruction through an old-fashioned medium: the mail. In all, Kaczynski's mail bombs killed three people and injured another 23. During this time, the Unabomber had spent his days in an out-of-the-way Montana cabin, constructing bombs for his enemies and writing his manifesto, in which he railed against the evils of postmodern, technology-dependent America (Figure 5.3 shows the pieces of shrapnel that were recovered from the Unabomber's February 1987 bombing at the CAAMS Inc. computer store in Salt Lake City, Utah).

Kaczynski's manifesto was printed in its entirety—just as he had demanded—in the *Washington Post*, where it accomplished a twofold purpose (Fox, Levin, and Fridel, 2018). First, from the point of view of the killer, it made the Unabomber into a kind of folk hero and cemented the image of a well-meaning if misguided humanitarian who dedicated his life to saving people from themselves. Indeed, Americans organized Unabomber fan clubs and defense funds; they wore Unabomber T-shirts and they watched as comedian Jay Leno participated in Unabomber skits on his nightly TV show.

From the viewpoint of the FBI, however, printing the manifesto had a different result: namely, providing readers with a set of clues that they

**Figure 5.3:** Image of shrapnel from a 1987 Unabomber attack

Source: U.S. Federal Bureau of Investigation/Wikimedia Commons

might recognize as associated with someone they knew and ultimately contributing to the Unabomber's capture. Sure enough, the Unabomber's brother, David Kaczynski, easily recognized certain idiosyncrasies in the syntax and substance of the manifesto, and reported this information to the FBI. Thanks to a family that turned in one of its own in order to save the lives of total strangers, Theodore Kaczynski was arrested in April 1996 and convicted of multiple counts of murder and the transportation, mailing, and use of bombs. He received multiple life sentences in prison with no possibility of parole. In June 2023, the 81-year-old inmate died by suicide.

## The future of covert warfare?

Over the course of the 20th century, Japan, Russia, and Germany demonstrated their capacity for enacting surprise attacks, and America responded with a program of its own. By June 1944, the United States had stockpiled anthrax and botulinum toxin in large enough quantities to permit effective retaliation in the event of a biological strike by foreign forces. For the same reason, the British tested anthrax bombs off the coast of Scotland in 1942 and 1943, and then stockpiled anthrax-infested cattle feed that could be used to taint an enemy food source. From 1951 to 1954, the American military released benign organisms off both U.S. coasts to give an idea of the weakness of American cities to biological attacks from foreign lands. In 1966, the same vulnerability was assessed by releasing a harmless test substance into the New York City subway system.

Fortunately, a biological attack on U.S. cities perpetrated by America's enemies never came to pass, yet the menace of biological warfare remains.

Moreover, as seen in the January 2021 siege of the U.S. Capitol, domestic terrorism continues to be a threat to the nation. It has been more than two decades since the World Health Organization declared that smallpox, an extremely contagious and incurable disease, had been eliminated, yet frozen quantities of the smallpox virus continue to be stored by the U.S. and Russian governments. Obviously, there could be catastrophic consequences if duplicitous domestic politicians or political leaders in "rogue states" (for example, Iraq or North Korea) find a way of obtaining such stocks of the disease.

The widespread outbreak of a deadly and easily transmittable illness could severely curtail the military superiority of the United States and other worldwide powers. Though lacking credible evidence, there still are conspiracy theorists who believe that the deadly SARS-CoV-2 virus (which causes the disease known as COVID-19), which led to an ongoing global pandemic beginning in 2020, was a deliberate act of bio-terrorism by Chinese scientists working in a Wuhan lab. Whatever its actual source—natural, accidental, or manufactured—it's clear that the virus has been responsible for millions of deaths worldwide. Moreover, it raises the specter of possible acts of biological warfare in the future. If the fundamental characteristics of covert violence hold true, such an attack would most likely come from an under-resourced and power-deprived group or nation. As biophysicist Steven Block (2001, p. 33) suggested, biological weapons may very well be "the poor man's atom bomb."

## References

Atwood, K. (2021). CIA launches task force to probe invisible attacks on U.S. diplomats and spies as one victim finds some relief. *CNN*. https://www.cnn.com/2021/02/24/politics/cia-diplomats-sonic-attacks-task-force/index.html

Baxter, R.R., and Buergenthal, T. (1970). Legal aspects of the Geneva Protocol of 1925. *American Journal of International Law 64*(5), 853–879.

Block, S.M. (2001). The growing threat of biological weapons. *American Scientist 89*(1), 28–37.

Curtis, M., and Kennard, M. (2019, September 17). Britain's seven covert wars: An explainer. *Declassified UK*. https://www.dailymaverick.co.za/article/2019-09-17-britains-seven-covert-wars-an-explainer/

Dobbs, M. (2004). *Saboteurs: The Nazi raid on America*. Knopf.

FBI. (n.d.). *Nazi saboteurs and George Dasch*. https://www.fbi.gov/history/famous-cases/nazi-saboteurs-and-george-dasch

Fox, J., Levin, J., and Fridel, E. (2018). *Extreme killing: Understanding serial and mass murder* (4th ed.). Sage Publications.

Frischknecht, F. (2003). The history of biological warfare: Human experimentation, modern nightmares, and lone madmen in the twentieth century. *EMBO Reports, 4*, S47–S52. https://www.ncbi.nlm.nih.gov/pmc/articles/PMC1326439/

History.com editors. (2009, October 14). Battle of the Bulge. https://www.history.com/topics/world-war-ii/battle-of-the-bulge

Kiner, D. (2020, December 16). "The greatest American battle": The Battle of the Bulge in World War II started 76 years ago. *The Patriot-News*. https://www.pennlive.com/nation-world/2020/12/the-greatest-american-battle-the-battle-of-the-bulge-in-world-war-ii.html

Kristof, N.D. (1995, March 17). Unmasking horror—a special report: Japan confronting gruesome war atrocity. *New York Times*. https://www.nytimes.com/1995/03/17/world/unmasking-horror-a-special-report-japan-confronting-gruesome-war-atrocity.html

Levin, J. (2006). *Domestic terrorism*. Chelsea Publications.

MacQueen, G. (2014). *The 2001 anthrax deception*. Clarity Press.

Record, J. (2005). Why the strong lose. *Parameters 35*(4), 16–31. https://press.armywarcollege.edu/cgi/viewcontent.cgi?article=2281&context=parameters

Roth, A. (2021, February 3). Alexei Navalny: 1,000 arrested after protests over jailing of Russian opposition leader. *The Guardian*. https://www.theguardian.com/world/2021/feb/02/russian-opposition-leader-alexei-navalny-jailed

Shane, S., and Zarate, A. (2006, June 24). FBI killed plot in talking stage, a top aide says. *New York Times*. https://www.nytimes.com/2006/06/24/us/24terror.html

Vergara, E. (2019, January 30). Chilean judge sentences 6 people in ex-president's death. *Associated Press*. https://apnews.com/article/740065eb3ad446b7b7127a5b1e82a637

Willman, D. (2011). *The mirage man: Bruce Ivins, the anthrax attacks, and America's rush to war*. Random House.

Zhang, S. (2016, November 22). How DNA evidence confirmed a Soviet cover-up of an anthrax accident. *The Atlantic*. https://www.theatlantic.com/health/archive/2016/11/sverdlovsk-russia-anthrax/508139/

6

# Healthcare

Hospitals, nursing homes, and other medical facilities are potential hotbeds for covert violence, if for no other reason than the fact that many, many people die there every year. After all, patients typically check into a hospital because of serious illness or injury, and nursing homes are intended for those who need round-the-clock care. Although most of the sick and injured who seek medical care in the United States and elsewhere are treated and then released on the road to recovery, many others die on the operating table or in their hospital bed. Death is very much part of life in healthcare facilities, which unfortunately also makes them places where a killer can operate unnoticed for long periods of time without being discovered.

According to the Centers for Disease Control and Prevention (CDC), diseases, illnesses, and other naturally occurring medical conditions account for more than 90 percent of U.S. deaths each year, with a large proportion of those occurring in medical facilities (although at lower rates than in the past, as greater awareness of palliative care and concern for patient preferences have resulted in more people dying in their own homes; see Shmerling [2018]). Add to that U.S. deaths from accidents (the third-highest cause of U.S. deaths), assaults, and complications of medical and surgical care—many of which also occur in medical facilities—and the death toll seems staggering. With nearly three million total U.S. deaths a year (Xu et al., 2021) and more than 700,000 people dying annually in hospitals (Shmerling, 2018), it seems reasonable to estimate that at least one million deaths collectively occur in U.S. healthcare facilities each year.

The lack of clear data related to medical deaths is an enormous obstacle preventing better understanding of the covert violence that occurs in these settings. The CDC recorded 5,329 U.S. deaths in 2019 that were caused by "complications of medical and surgical care" (Xu et al., 2021). This category includes deaths from medical devices, adverse effects related to incorrect doses of therapeutic medications, and difficulties that arose during surgical or medical care. However, deaths from *accidental* overdoses of a drug or from drugs administered *in error* are excluded here, even when they occurred in a healthcare setting and/or the drugs were administered by a doctor or other healthcare professional.

Accidental medical deaths are instead added to the total of accidental deaths in all settings, which the CDC reported was 173,040 in 2019. From there, it's difficult to extrapolate just how many were medically related, though a little deductive reasoning can provide a clue: out of the 173,040 accidental deaths recorded in 2019, subtracting 39,107 that were attributed to motor vehicle crashes, 39,443 from falls, 486 from firearm discharges, 3,692 from drownings, 7,076 from suffocation, 2,692 from exposure to smoke/fire, and 65,773 from poisonings leaves 14,771 deaths in the subcategory "other and unspecified non-transport accidents and their sequelae." Thus, the number of U.S. deaths because of medical errors in 2019 seems to be some figure that is less than 14,771.

However, a recent study by researchers at the Yale School of Medicine (Rodwin et al., 2020) offers another perspective by estimating the number of hospital deaths that were *preventable*, putting that figure at about 22,165 each year in the United States. The reason why that number is higher than the CDC's figure (whatever it may be) is because the researchers' definition of *preventable hospital death* is more inclusive than the CDC's definition of *medical accidents*. In other words, the estimated number of preventable hospital deaths includes at least some of the cases that the CDC classifies as "complications of medical and surgical care." Interestingly, the Yale study also provides an estimated breakdown of the percent of preventable hospital deaths according to the expected longevity of the patients, noting that the majority (about 68 percent) occurred among patients who were expected to live only another three months or less. This seems to increase the likelihood that at least some deaths of this sort are classified by the CDC as from natural causes—particularly when those patients are elderly.

Further complicating the search for reliable information on U.S. deaths is the fact that there are multiple sources of official data, which frequently contain contradictions. Scientific studies have found substantial inaccuracies on death certificates when comparing them to the same patients' medical charts. One recent study that focused on inpatient hospital death rates in the St. Louis and Kansas City metropolitan areas in Missouri reported that "an average of 45.8 percent of reviewed death certificates were completed incorrectly" (Lloyd et al., 2017, p. 21). The investigators recommended additional training for those completing the documents, as the information is vital for the development of nationwide healthcare policies and priorities—and for truly understanding how and why people die in healthcare settings.

Another recent study (Miller et al., 2022)—this one examining hospital discharge data related to firearm injuries, not deaths—found a large number of medical coding errors that might signal additional problems. A team of medical practitioners and researchers studied the accuracy of how firearm-related injuries had been classified by intent (that is, assault, self-harm, accident, legal intervention, or undetermined cause) in discharge data at three U.S. hospitals from 2008 to 2019. Not only did findings reveal "substantial" misclassification in firearm injury intent data entered by medical records coders, but they also specifically indicated that the predominant error was coding firearm injuries as accidents that actually resulted from assaults—nearly 30 percent of assault-related cases were misclassified in this way. Reliance on these data, then, would inflate the incidence of accidental firearm injuries while undercounting those resulting from assaults.

Beyond inexact and inconsistent data, the exact reason for many deaths that occur in hospitals and nursing homes is also frequently unclear. Many people who are admitted to hospitals and nursing homes arrive with a mix of illnesses, any one of which could become out of control or cause a change in the status of another. Plus, in cases where a patient's illnesses span multiple specialties, they may be under the care of several doctors who don't necessarily come together to fully understand the patient's overall health and coordinate care. This can easily lead to dangerous drug interactions, improper diagnoses, and counterproductive treatments that contribute to deaths that are not well understood. Add to this the inevitable complications and resulting deaths because of human error (that is, medical mistakes), and it seems clear that there is far more nuance surrounding medically related deaths than many people would guess.

It is also worth noting that medical staff have a vested interest in *not* clearly identifying mistakes and in *not* uncovering intentional malevolence, especially if there is little evidence present or when the situation is reasonably ambiguous. After all, mishaps and misdeeds can both result in expensive lawsuits, licensure suspensions, staff layoffs, and/or facility shutdowns. Even the resulting media attention could prove detrimental, as would-be patients decide not to risk being treated at *the hospital that made a mistake* or *the clinic that used to employ a killer.*

Moreover, when a family member or friend suspects that a hospital or nursing home staff member has intentionally harmed or taken the life of their loved one, how would they go about proving it? When a frail and sickly patient suddenly stops breathing, it may not be possible to definitively determine what exactly caused their death. Did they expire from natural causes or were they suffocated with a pillow? Certain poisons inserted into a patient's IV or injected between their toes may be difficult or impossible to detect, even following an autopsy. Indeed, depending on the age and health conditions of a patient, it may never occur to anyone in charge to look for evidence of foul play. When it comes to ambiguous deaths, those resulting from an accident, natural causes, and malevolence can all look identical.

Where technology like cameras may help to prevent or prosecute crimes in other arenas of social life, many forms of surveillance are prohibited in medical settings, as per the Health Insurance Portability and Accountability Act (HIPAA). While the law provides important privacy protections for patients, it may also inadvertently contribute to concealing covert acts of violence that take place in healthcare facilities.

## Powerless perpetrators who prey on patients

In hospitals, nursing homes, and other healthcare facilities, physicians rarely commit medical murder. They tend to hold much more powerful and prestigious positions compared to orderlies, nurse's aides, and even nurses. Medical doctors—especially those with a certified specialty—enjoy enormous amounts of economic power, with large salaries that are projected to increase at a faster clip in the next few years (Keehan et al., 2020). As an additional source of income, about 47 percent of U.S. physicians as of 2016 had an ownership stake in the medical practices in which they work (Kane, 2017). In addition to enjoying the kinds of personal power that often accompany economic clout (such as having more autonomy, control, and flexibility in daily life than most other people), physicians also tend to be treated with admiration and respect, are generally assumed to be competent and intelligent, and are rarely questioned or doubted.

Such large repositories of power, however, could provide added cover for physicians with nefarious intentions. That was the case with the English doctor Harold Shipman (discussed in Chapter 1), who murdered at least 15 patients under his care, mostly by injecting a lethal dose of a powerful narcotic. Indeed, it was Shipman's powerful professional status that both enabled his crimes and helped to conceal them. As a doctor, he was afforded easy access to his victims and their medical records—which he would alter to indicate natural causes for the deaths—as well as their trust and consent to receive medical treatment (which could reasonably include injections) and the implicit trust of patients' families, hospital staff, and any other potential observers.

On the other hand, orderlies and nurse's aides hold very little power—certainly far less than physicians and nurses, but also somewhat less than patients. For meager salaries, much of their work is menial (for example, transporting patients, cleaning rooms, and sterilizing medical equipment), while some is downright unpleasant (for example, cleaning soiled bedding, emptying bedpans, and giving sponge baths). Their workdays are structured by more powerful others, who dictate most aspects of their time, attire, language, and movement. And these employees frequently report demanding and disrespectful treatment by patients, as well as ambivalence from many higher-powered colleagues.

On occasion, these powerless medical members of staff decide to take action themselves and seize the power that they have been consistently denied. Few will target the top rungs of the medical authority hierarchy, such as hospital administrators and physicians, and instead will make victims of those to whom they have more ready access: patients. Some of them aim to "play God" by usurping the role of physicians and taking advantage of their occupational invisibility to decide which patients will live and which will die. For them, it is a way to prove their ability to take control—not only to control the life or death of another person, but also to take charge of the life-saving decision-making authority that is afforded to doctors and nurses.

An infamous example is that of orderly Donald Harvey, who took the lives of more than three dozen patients (he claimed a total of 87) while working in hospitals in Kentucky and Ohio from 1970 to 1987. After he was arrested, Harvey became known as the "Angel of Death" because he claimed that his intentions were merciful and only meant to end the suffering of chronically ill patients. (The moniker references religious imagery of a benevolent being who helps those who are sick and suffering transition to the afterlife, as depicted in Figure 6.1, and has been applied to other covert killers in healthcare settings.) However, his usual methods would have been brutally painful, and not all his victims were patients or even sick, as they also included a live-in lover and two neighbors. Although he occasionally suffocated patients—smothering some with a pillow or plastic bag and depriving others of life-sustaining oxygen—he preferred poisoning them, usually with cyanide or arsenic, but sometimes by administering an overdose of insulin or morphine. When he was finally caught 17 years after his first killing , Harvey pleaded guilty to a total of 37 murders and received multiple life sentences, which he was ordered to serve in Ohio. He died in March 2017 at the age of 64 after a brutal beating by a fellow inmate in the prison's protective custody unit.

Medical institutions housing frail and elderly patients are especially likely to be targeted by powerless members of staff. In the 1980s, two nurse's aides at a suburban Grand Rapids, Michigan, nursing home killed five patients by smothering them. The women were romantically involved and may have planned the murders as part of a "lovers' pact." Much like the initiation rituals of gangs and fraternities that purport to prove a prospective member's loyalty to the group—taking a beating, attacking a rival, or enduring emotional abuse and humiliation—lovers, too, have been known to commit abhorrent acts for the purpose of sealing their shared loyalty and dedication to one another.

In 1986, while working at the Alpine Manor Nursing Home in Walker, Michigan, 26-year-old Catherine May ("Cathy") Wood left her husband, Kenneth, and her six-year-old daughter to establish a lesbian relationship with fellow nurse's aide, 25-year-old Gwendolyn ("Gwen") Graham, who had recently moved to the area from Tyler, Texas. Over a two-month period

**Figure 6.1:** Image of Evelyn De Morgan's 1881 painting, "Angel of Death"

Source: Melesse/Wikimedia Commons

in 1987, the women took the lives of five elderly patients, most of whom suffered from Alzheimer's disease (Fox, Levin, and Fridel, 2018).

The two killers divided the labor between them. Wood was the lookout, keeping watch from the door of the ward as Graham smothered each patient by placing a washcloth over her nose and mouth. Only very frail and sickly victims—those who could be easily overpowered—were chosen. The pair's selection of victims was strategic in a few other ways, too. First, killing only those who were very ill and weak allowed them to convince themselves that the murders were really mercy killings designed to alleviate the patients' pain and suffering. The pair also decided to select victims by playing a vile game in which they sought out patients whose first-name initials would collectively spell out the word "M–U–R–D–E–R," a method that, in their twisted minds, left up to fate or chance the choice of exactly who would die. Lastly, the high prevalence of severe illness and death in nursing homes reduced the likelihood that other staff members or the patients' family would suspect foul play.

For Wood and Graham, the secrecy of their complicity in the killings secured their bond and would prevent either of them from abandoning the relationship. However, the killing couple later went their separate ways when Graham started dating another female nurse's aide at Alpine Manor and then relocated with her back to Texas, where she got a job at a hospital caring for infants. In the meantime, Wood confessed the morbid details of the murders to the Michigan authorities (after being compelled by her ex-husband, whom she told first) and subsequently agreed to a plea deal that reduced her charges in exchange for testifying against Graham, who was charged with five counts of first-degree murder.

At trial, Wood testified that it was Graham who had planned and carried out the killings while she merely served as a lookout. The authenticity of Wood's allegations was enhanced by the testimony of Graham's new girlfriend, who claimed under oath that Graham had confessed the killings to her. In November 1989, Graham was given five life sentences and sent to the Women's Huron Valley Correctional Facility in Michigan. For her role, Wood received a sentence of 40 years in a minimum-security federal prison in Florida for one count of second-degree murder and one count of conspiracy to commit second-degree murder. She first became eligible for parole in 2005 and was denied several times, until she was eventually released in January 2020. As part of the terms of her release, she was ordered to stay away from the elderly, children, and other "vulnerable adults." She reportedly moved to Fort Mill, South Carolina, to live with her sister (Baker, 2020).

## Saving lives and taking lives

Nearly all healthcare-related murders with multiple victims have taken place within a hospital or nursing home setting, with only a handful occurring in patients' homes (Frieden, 2014). That could soon change, however, with the increasing emphasis on palliative care in the United States that has resulted in more people with terminal illnesses choosing to die in the comfort of their own homes (Shmerling, 2018). In many of these cases, the family employs the services of home-healthcare professionals to provide constant care and monitoring for their dying loved one. Yet, these professionals tend to work alone and spend their time rotating through the homes of several regular patients at any given time, often resulting in a great deal of one-on-one time between the worker and patient inside a private residence. Certainly, most home-healthcare workers are well-trained and well-intentioned professionals, but if *even one* has murderous intentions, patients' own homes could provide sufficient cover to conceal the actions of a covert killer for quite some time.

Medical killers have used a variety of covert methods of murder, but poisoning via medications is the most common, usually injecting it into an IV or directly into a patient. Again, a variety of medications have been used for this purpose, but the most common ones include opioids and opiates, potassium chloride, insulin, muscle relaxants, sedatives, heart drugs, and blood thinners. Most drugs used to poison patients are taken clandestinely, either through legitimate means or by theft, from the facility pharmacy or storeroom. Others who lack access to drugs or prefer other methods have used chemicals such as bleach, an empty needle to inject air into a blood vessel and cause an air embolism, smothering or suffocation, water in the lungs, and equipment tampering.

Covert killers in healthcare settings tend to operate alone, though not all, as illustrated in the "Lethal Lovers" case of Cathy Wood and Gwen Graham. They exhibit few reliable warning signs and leave few reliable clues. They tend to move around—from job to job, hospital to hospital, and/or state to state—making their detection much more difficult. Some might act strangely at the death of a patient, seem to enjoy the attention they get from colleagues and families upon a patient's death, and/or have a record of discipline for low-level infractions. Then again, some might have exemplary records and reputations. Such characteristics may seem indicative of deviant motivation and behavior, but they are hardly emblematic of murderous intentions. Indeed, countless healthcare workers who possess similar traits never harm anyone (Yardley and Wilson, 2014).

To the naïve observer, those who murder multiple helpless patients who are weak and suffering may seem to be altruistic and enacting the ultimate version of merciful euthanasia. Yet, this is very rarely, if ever, what drives these despicable acts. Their motivation is much more sinister. They kill to gain the sense of control, dominance, and power that they crave but find consistently lacking in their everyday role as lower-status healthcare workers. It allows them to rob the high-powered doctors of their life-saving decision-making authority on their own home turf. In cases where murder becomes addictive, the death toll can be enormous—dozens of elderly and infirm patients slain in a mysterious manner while the murderous staffer was on duty. When the body count reaches multiple numbers, the caretaker-lifetakers often are labeled in the news media as "Angels of Death" to emphasize their astounding misdeeds and apparently warped sense of justice.

Thirty-eight-year-old Orville Lynn Majors may have been deserving of the label "Angel of Death." Working for almost two years as a nurse in the intensive care unit of Vermillion County Hospital in Clinton, Indiana, about 60 miles west of Indianapolis, 147 patients died, most of them while he was on shift. In 1995, hospital administrators asked the police to investigate after a hospital supervisor's study found that the intensive care unit's death rate had risen to 120 a year in 1994 from 31 or fewer annually earlier in the decade. The number of deaths especially increased when Majors was working with patients in the unit; therefore, in the interests of caution, he was suspended with pay (Levin, 2008).

As soon as Majors was labeled a person of interest, it seems that he became regarded as guilty in the court of public opinion. Thus, every idiosyncrasy of the suspect that was formerly overlooked came to be seen by the victims' families as a red flag. They apparently now thought that he was strange, that he acted bizarrely, that his smile appeared evil, that he had temper tantrums, that he was a loner, that he had an emotionless blank stare, and that overall he was just a weird fellow. Prior to officially labeling the nurse as a possible killer, the same characteristics easily passed for "normal." But, once someone becomes a person of interest in a murder case, all who suspected them seem to suddenly recognize all the warning signs they had missed beforehand.

At this point, none of the families' accusations against Majors had been substantiated, and he had not been officially charged with any crime. But the deaths had occurred unexpectedly on his shifts, and he had been observed by family members as working in proximity to some patients just prior to their deaths. Moreover, a few of the deadly injections were purportedly witnessed by family members who had visited loved ones in the hospital. The son of one victim said about Majors: "I saw him inject my dad in the heart area, and my dad passed away within a minute or so, that quick" (Levin, 2008, p. 47). After 15 bodies were exhumed for further testing, the authorities discovered that at least six deaths could be attributed to poisoning via injection of epinephrine and potassium chloride, drugs that were later found in Majors' possession.

Regarding Majors' complicity, the "red flags" turned out to be accurate indicators. In December 1997, he was arrested and charged with the seven patient murders for which the prosecution had the strongest evidence. During the trial, a former roommate testified that Majors had told him that he hated old people and thought that "they should all be gassed." Majors had chosen death for those patients he considered to be incessantly demanding and those he felt complained in a whiny and annoying manner.

In October 1999, Majors was found guilty of the premeditated murders of four women and two men, ages 56–89, who died between 1993 and 1995. He was sentenced to serve 360 years in prison. Moreover, some 80 family members of patients who had met mysterious deaths filed wrongful-death lawsuits against him and the hospital. The hospital was fined $80,000 by the State of Indiana for negligence and code violations and was subsequently renamed and leased to a private company. In September 2017, while serving time at the Indiana State Prison in Michigan City, Majors complained of having difficulty breathing and subsequently became unresponsive. Shortly thereafter, he died of natural causes involving a heart condition at 56 years old. All told, Majors was linked to about 130 deaths, but was never tried for most of his crimes.

Official U.S. crime statistics have consistently shown that men commit acts of violence and murder at far higher rates than women. Yet, this longstanding trend may only hold for cases of *overt* violence, as vastly more women appear to commit *covert* acts of violence than experts would have previously thought. Moreover, professions that traditionally have been dominated by women— especially nursing, social work, and other so-called helping professions—also show greater numbers of female perpetrators. Within healthcare settings, we find similar percentages of women and men who become prolific medical killers using covert methods. However, this is likely to be related to the fact that women not only outnumber men in these settings, but also that their numbers tend to be concentrated in less powerful positions (for example, nurses and nurse's aides) compared to men.

One trend that continues to hold is that, unlike their male counterparts, female killers' quest for power does not usually involve sexual sadism. Instead, these women tend to derive personal satisfaction from being in control of deciding who should live or die in a situation where not everyone can be saved, and such decisions are potentially plentiful in healthcare settings. Moreover, physical power is often less relevant in medical situations. While many women might have more difficulty than their male counterparts subduing a healthy victim using brute force, it takes much less strength and physical effort to overpower a defenseless patient in a hospital or nursing home, especially if the victim is already near death. Also, while men more often kill overtly with brute force, women have long been known to use more passive-aggressive means, such as medicines, poisons, and suffocation. It should not be surprising, then, that female nurses and nurse's aides are especially likely to use covert methods to attack patients who are simply too weak and frail to defend themselves.

During the seven years she worked as a nurse at the Veterans Administration (VA) Hospital in Northampton, Massachusetts, 30-year-old Kristen Gilbert had been on duty for almost half of the 350 deaths that occurred in her unit. This fact went unnoticed until February 1996, when multiple patients suffered cardiac arrest in the intensive care unit, all on Gilbert's 4pm-to-midnight shift, and three nurses reported concerns about a surge of cardiac arrest deaths and an unexpected decrease in the supply of epinephrine, also known as adrenaline. A formal investigation determined that Gilbert had injected six patients with overdoses of epinephrine, which sped up their heart rates to dangerous levels. Her intention was apparently to place herself in the middle of medical emergencies so that she could attract the attention and admiration of her lover, a hospital security officer with whom she was having an affair. Four of the overdosed patients had fatal heart attacks, while the other two were fortunate enough to recover.

Gilbert was suspected in the deaths of dozens more patients, but there was never enough evidence to charge her with them. There were, of course, plenty of circumstantial reasons to suspect her. In her role as a nurse, she had easily secured bottles of epinephrine from the hospital storage room. She was the first medical practitioner to be on the scene at every one of the deaths. And she resigned from her position at the hospital around the same time that the outbreak of mysterious deaths ended. Gilbert ended up admitting the killings to her then-boyfriend and her estranged husband, both of whom later testified against her in court.

By September 1996, the relationship between Gilbert and her boyfriend had soured, and bomb threats began. During the month, her boyfriend received several phone calls from someone who anonymously claimed to have planted bombs at the VA Hospital, where he provided security. Patients were evacuated, no explosives were discovered, and investigators eventually traced the phone calls to Gilbert. She was convicted in January 1998 of making bomb threats and sentenced to 15 months in prison. Meanwhile, investigators were coming closer and closer to connecting Gilbert to the patient deaths.

The evidence was ultimately overwhelming. In March 2001, a federal jury convicted Gilbert on three counts of first-degree murder, one count of second-degree murder, and two counts of attempted murder. Jurors recommended a sentence of life in prison, and the judge responded by ordering four consecutive life terms without the possibility of parole, plus an additional 20 years. Gilbert is currently serving her time at the Federal Medical Center, Carswell in Fort Worth, Texas.

Most medical killers want nothing more than to cause the untimely death of their patients. For pediatric nurse Genene Jones, causing a life-or-death emergency was a means to an end, as it provided an opportunity to be a hero—to intervene in the nick of time, save the life of her victim, and receive commendations from colleagues and members of the patient's family. Sadly, her plan to become a local hero didn't always leave her victims alive. From May to December 1981, ten children in the intensive care unit of Bexar County Hospital in San Antonio, Texas, suddenly stopped breathing and died, all during Jones' shift.

Although inconclusive, a hospital investigation could not rule out negligence or wrongdoing on the part of Jones, and she resigned from her position at Bexar County Hospital in March 1982. Despite being suspected of causing the unexplained deaths, she was given a letter of recommendation from her former employer that described her as an "asset" to the hospital district and characterized her as "loyal, dependable, and trustworthy." Shortly thereafter, she began working at a pediatrician's clinic in Kerrville, some 60 miles northwest of San Antonio.

One of Jones' first patients was Chelsea Ann McClellan, a 15-month-old girl whose mother had brought her to the clinic for a routine examination. While Dr. Kathleen Holland, the physician in charge, conferred with the baby's mother, Jones waited with Chelsea in an adjoining examining room. It was only a few moments until the nurse was heard crying out that the tiny patient had stopped breathing and was in dire need of an ambulance. Accompanying little Chelsea on the way to the hospital, Jones worked hard to revive her patient. When she succeeded and the child regained consciousness, her parents were understandably elated and spread the word about the wonderful new nurse in town who had saved their daughter's life. As a result, Jones became an instant hero in the local community.

Unfortunately, the good news didn't last long. A few weeks later, little Chelsea returned to the clinic for a follow-up examination with Dr. Holland. On this second visit, just after nurse Jones gave the child an injection in each thigh that she said were immunizations, she once again stopped breathing and began to have a seizure. Jones again accompanied the young patient in the ambulance to the hospital, but this time Chelsea died en route. Suspicions about Jones grew over the next several months, especially when other children also stopped breathing after visiting the clinic and had to be rushed to the hospital, and when Dr. Holland found that a bottle of Anectine, a powerful muscle relaxant, appeared to have been tampered with, it was eventually enough to compel the exhumation of Chelsea's body, and an autopsy confirmed the presence of Anectine.

In February 1984, Jones was convicted of killing Chelsea and sentenced to 99 years in prison. Later that year, she was also convicted in another case of causing injury to a child and given a concurrent sentence of 60 years. In order to prevent her impending mandatory release from prison, Jones was charged in 2017 in the deaths of five babies from her time working at Bexar County Hospital in the 1980s. In January 2020, as part of a plea bargain in which four of the charges were dropped, Jones pleaded guilty to the murder of 11-month-old Joshua Sawyer and received a life sentence. She must serve 18 years of that sentence before becoming eligible for parole at the age of 87.

## Some positive signs for the future

Recent changes in healthcare operations have helped to reduce the incidence of covert violence in U.S. healthcare settings, and additional changes are likely to occur that will make patients even safer. According to Dr. Eindra Khin

Khin, a psychiatrist whose specialties include criminal competency, criminal responsibility, and violence risk assessment, one of the primary reasons for the decrease in medical killers is the implementation of electronic medical records (EMR). In an interview for *MedPage Today* (Frieden, 2014), Khin Khin explained: "You can't just take out medications and start injecting someone; everyone's accountable because of EMR. But in most parts of the world, they don't even have EMR." This, she said, is one reason why many healthcare facilities outside of the United States have experienced the opposite trend—an increase in medical murders—in recent years. Also contributing to the global rise is what she described as a failure to keep up with implementing new credentialing guidelines and regulatory measures (Frieden, 2014).

Scholarly research also offers insights into potential ways for identifying medical killers more quickly. One study that analyzed a sample of nurses who killed two or more patients in hospitals (Yardley and Wilson, 2014) identified commonalities among these killers that should be considered "red flags," though they also cautioned against treating any one of them as definitive evidence of wrongdoing. The most common characteristics were: "higher incidences of death on his/her shift; history of mental instability/depression; makes colleagues anxious; in possession of drugs etc. at home/in locker; and appears to have a personality disorder" (Yardley and Wilson, 2014, p. 52).

Another potentially promising change is simply requiring healthcare workers to perform their duties in teams, including a mandate that no staff member may be alone with a patient, as well as a low-risk method for reporting rule violators. This would increase worker accountability and eliminate many opportunities for patient mistreatment. The team approach would be even more effective if it includes representation from a variety of staff positions (to limit an us-versus-them mentality that often perpetuates a cycle of silence) and if members are periodically rotated among assigned teams (to help reduce the development of group-related pressures that can lead to mistakes, oversights, or misguided loyalties). This change would also help to reduce covert violence by home healthcare workers who may be presently unaccompanied when making visits, as well as medical mistakes that currently account for thousands of American deaths each year.

## References

Baker, K.C. (2020, January 21). Female serial killer who murdered patients with Alzheimer's, dementia released after nearly 30 years. *People*. https://people.com/crime/female-serial-killer-who-murdered-patients-with-alzheimers-dementia-released-after-nearly-30-years/

Fox, J.A., Levin, J. and Fridel, E. (2018). *Extreme Killing: Understanding Serial and Mass Murder*. Sage.

Frieden, J. (2014, October 28). Healthcare serial killings down in U.S. but up globally: Electronic health records may be a deterrent. *MedPage Today.* https://www.medpagetoday.com/psychiatry/generalpsychiatry/48281

Kane, C.K. (2017). *Updated data on physician practice arrangements: Physician ownership drops below 50 percent.* American Medical Association. https://www.ama-assn.org/sites/ama-assn.org/files/corp/media-browser/public/health-policy/PRP-2016-physician-benchmark-survey.pdf

Keehan, S.P., Cuckler, G.A., Poisal, J.A., Sisko, A.M., Smith, S.D., Madison, A.J., et al. (2020). National health expenditure projections, 2019–28: Expected rebound in prices drives rising spending growth. *Health Affairs, 39*(4), 704–714.

Levin, J. (2008). *Serial killers and sadistic murderers—up close and personal.* Prometheus Books.

Lloyd, J., Jahanpour, E., Angell, B., Ward, C., Hunter, A., Baysinger, C., et al. (2017). Using national inpatient death rates as a benchmark to identify hospitals with inaccurate cause of death reporting—Missouri, 2009–2012. *Morbidity and Mortality Weekly Report, 66*(1), 19–22.

Miller, M., Azrael, D., Yenduri, R., Barber, C., Bowen, A., MacPhaul, E., et al. (2022). Assessment of accuracy of firearm injury intent coding at 3 US hospitals. *JAMA Network Open, 5*(12), 1–10. doi:10.1001/jamanetwork open.2022.46429

Rodwin, B.A., Bilan, V.P., Merchant, N.B., Steffens, C.G., Grimshaw, A.A., Bastian, L.A., et al. (2020). Rate of preventable mortality in hospitalized patients: A systematic review and meta-analysis. *Journal of General Internal Medicine, 35*(7), 2099–2106.

Shmerling, R.H. (2018, October 31). *Where people die.* Harvard Health Publishing. https://www.health.harvard.edu/blog/where-people-die-2018103115278

Xu, J., Murphy, S.L., Kochanek, K.D., and Arias, E. (2021). Deaths: Final data for 2019. *National Vital Statistics Reports, 70*(8). https://www.cdc.gov/nchs/data/nvsr/nvsr70/nvsr70-08-508.pdf

Yardley, E., and Wilson, D. (2014). In search of the "Angels of Death": Conceptualizing the contemporary nurse healthcare serial killer. *Journal of Investigative Psychology and Offender Profiling, 13*, 39–55.

# 7

# Mass Media

When thinking about violence against members of the mass media, the cases that tend to come to mind are those with the most famous victims, the most brazen perpetrators, and the most bizarre details. These cases involve mostly overt methods that frequently begin with an innocent-seeming initial contact before escalating over time to stalking behaviors and eventually one or more attempted or completed physical attacks, perhaps with a firearm or a knife. Indeed, numerous entertainers have been subjected to potentially violent stalkers. Media personalities are at particular risk for being stalked partly because of their high profile, but also because their role—whether they happen to be an entertainer, news anchor, radio morning show host, or politician—requires them to pander to an audience and sustain public attention (Wilson et al., 2018).

Many people have sent fan mail to their favorite celebrities and/or reached out to them on social media, and some die-hard fans pay exorbitant sums of money for backstage passes and meet-and-greet events with A-list stars. Very few would ever attempt to get closer than that, and rarer still are the handful of deranged individuals out there who develop unhealthy obsessions with famous people that may lead to dangerous—and sometimes deadly—consequences. Among the most notorious of these incidents are the fatal shootings of singer John Lennon in 1980 by an angry Beatles fan, of actor and model Rebecca Schaeffer in 1989 by an obsessed devotee, and of singer Selena Quintanilla-Perez in 1995 by the former president of her fan club. Several laws and other practices changed in the 1990s (particularly in response to the death of Schaeffer, who was shot in the doorway of her home after the killer obtained her address via California Department of Motor Vehicles records) that have helped to prevent more of these incidents, though they certainly still occur.

In a recent example, up-and-coming singer Christina Grimmie (who finished in third place on season six of *The Voice*) was fatally shot in 2016 by an obsessed fan while the 22-year-old signed autographs after a concert in Orlando, Florida. Stalkers have broken into the homes of Sandra Bullock, Selena Gomez, and Jennifer Lopez; have trespassed on properties owned by

Kendall Jenner, Madonna, and Taylor Swift; and have sent unwanted letters and gifts to numerous others. Male celebrities are also sometimes targeted by stalkers: Justin Bieber received threats from a former inmate saying that he and an accomplice planned to castrate and murder the singer, and a woman who stalked late-night talk show host David Letterman for years was arrested at least eight times for trespassing on his property and even stole a Porsche from his driveway.

These are just a few examples of the kinds of overt violence inflicted on media stars. Most are probably familiar, as each received massive amounts of news coverage and public attention. They also include details that illustrate more typical kinds of celebrity stalker cases, such as the common use of firearms. Moreover, the perpetrators usually suffer from a serious mental illness, frequently schizophrenia and paranoia. Most are unable to engage in healthy relationships and tend to suffer from depression and low self-esteem. Over time, some of these stalkers convince themselves that they have a genuine relationship with the object of their obsessive fantasy. Although perhaps less publicized, covert violence is also used against media personalities and public figures with some regularity—but, unlike overtly violent acts, covert incidents are far more likely to be perpetrated by seemingly ordinary individuals with mental health in the normal range.

## The high price of a high profile

Psychiatrists have identified eight types of motivation among stalkers of celebrities and public figures (see Wilson et al., 2018). Those motivated by feelings of powerlessness most clearly fit into the "resentful" type, which is viewed as "the most concerning in terms of violence risk" (Wilson et al., 2018, p. 154). The "resentful" stalkers angrily lash out, often because of a perceived grievance, but sometimes in pursuit of a particular goal or agenda. Their powerlessness stems from an inability to settle the grievance or achieve the goal on their own, combined with a feeling that they have been ignored by those in power who could help them, but don't.

As their resentfulness simmers, their frustration may eventually boil over into a terrible act of violence. Many will use an overt method to lash out, and this is especially likely for perpetrators with a mental illness and others who have no plan for avoiding capture. Those with mental health in the normal range, however, are more likely to realize that careful planning and secret preparations would increase the chances of achieving their vengeful aims while simultaneously decreasing the odds of getting caught. They would also have a greater capacity for developing a rational plan, as well as the patience and self-control to wait for just the right moment to strike.

Some of the changed practices within the entertainment industry over the last 30 or so years have substantially reduced the likelihood that a celebrity will encounter an armed individual who intends them harm. It's more difficult to legally obtain the home address of a celebrity than it used to be, especially in California, and most stars hire bodyguards and maintain extensive home security systems. Further, most work in highly controlled environments (for example, recording studios, arenas, and film sets) that have their own security measures, including metal detectors to help keep weapons out. This has further increased the amount of power held by the biggest stars, as well as the likelihood that a powerless perpetrator will turn to covert methods to achieve their malicious aims.

After gaining international fame as the lead singer of the Icelandic alternative rock band The Sugarcubes, musician Björk moved to London in 1993 to begin her solo career. Her success took off from there and soon far surpassed that of her former band. Among Björk's numerous fans, at least one had developed an unhealthy fixation that steadily grew over several years before erupting into violence. Ricardo López was a 21-year-old Uruguayan-American living in Hollywood, Florida, and working in pest control. He was also fully consumed by his obsession with Björk, and the final straw appeared to be her new relationship with musician Goldie. In September 1996, López mailed a letter bomb rigged with sulfuric acid to Björk's London home and then took his own life. When his body was discovered a few days later, police also found a video diary that López had recorded over nine months that focused on his obsession with Björk and documented his suicide at the end. Officers were able to contact the British authorities in time to intercept the package before it ever reached the musician.

Although A-list celebrities and others with ample resources are better protected from violent stalkers today than in the past, the same is not necessarily true for less famous entertainers or for local-level celebrities and public figures. Anyone in the public eye is at risk, but the problem is especially pronounced for female news anchors and reporters. High-profile forensic psychiatrist Dr. Park Dietz was quoted in a *Psychology Today* article (Wise, 2010) as saying that being stalked is "virtually a certainty" for women in this field, adding: "At any given time, she might be stalked by several at once and not even know about it."

In a recent example, a Philadelphia man was convicted in February 2020 of stalking and harassing local NBC 10 news anchor Tracy Davidson over about a 26-month period. On multiple occasions between October 2017 and January 2019, 42-year-old David E. Silvan sent packages to Davidson's home that contained pornography, lingerie, and romantic letters. The lack of postage and writing on some packages made it clear that those had been hand-delivered, presumably by Silvan himself.

At the sentencing hearing the following June, the judge referred to Silvan as "a dangerous individual" and called his behavior "a very serious offense" before ordering him to serve between two and 23 months in the county jail. In addition, Silvan will have to complete five years of probation and could face additional jail time if he violates any of those terms, which include staying away from Davidson and her workplace and complying with all recommendations of a psychosexual evaluation. Davidson, who started working at the station in 1996, was not present at the sentencing hearing, but provided a statement to be read aloud in court. She wrote, in part: "I was shaken to my core. It was deviant material. The experience was frightening. The safety and security I always felt in my home was now shattered" (Hessler, 2020).

## Digital disguises

While measures to protect the physical safety of celebrities have increased, the rise of digital technologies has allowed for new methods of covert attack. Hiding in the shadows of the so-called *dark web*, under the shroud of anonymity are powerless individuals who have developed frightening new ways to threaten, harass, and assault the objects of their obsession. As digital technologies have become easier to use and simultaneously less expensive, access to them has increased dramatically around the world. This trend has expanded the availability of information, as well as options for communication, education, and employment, but these resources can be used for destructive purposes just as easily as productive ones.

The dark web, which is also sometimes referred to as the *deep web*, includes the various overlay networks called *darknets* that exist on the World Wide Web, but that cannot be accessed through mainstream means. These networks are invisible to search engines and require specific software, configurations, and/or authorizations to use. The most widely known vehicle for reaching the dark web is through the *Tor browser*, which is a free and open-source software that conceals the location and usage information of its users. Once on the dark web, social media platforms such as *4chan* and *8chan* allow for anonymous interactions and information sharing. Users are not required to reveal their real names, and posts are not necessarily tied to particular usernames or accounts, making the identification of individual posters very difficult.

This is a space where even A-listers remain at high risk. In the summer of 2014, for example, nude photos of several dozen female celebrities surfaced on the Reddit website after first being posted anonymously on 4chan (presumably by whoever hacked the victims' media in the first place). The images (the authenticity of which was questioned by some of the alleged victims) included those of Oscar-winner Jennifer Lawrence, models Kate Upton and Erin Heatherton, reality star Kim Kardashian, singer Rihanna, soccer player Hope Solo, and actors Gabrielle Union, Kirsten Dunst, Kaley Cuoco, and Mena Suvari.

The dark web—and 4chan in particular—is where the far-right extremist conspiracy theory known as *QAnon* began in the fall of 2017. What started as a series of posts by a user who signed off as "Q," the unfounded theory quickly spread among an underground community and by 2020 had at least hundreds of thousands of believers (Wendling, 2021). Basically, QAnon asserted that President Donald Trump was "waging a secret war against elite Satan-worshipping pedophiles in government, business, and the media" (Wendling, 2021), mostly targeting Democrats, journalists, and celebrities. Like other dark web activities that are meant to incite violence, QAnon posts are not just idle threats, but have led to actual violence.

Supporters have been arrested for multiple kidnappings, at least one murder, an armed standoff on a bridge near the Hoover Dam, and trespassing on the property of Canadian Prime Minister Justin Trudeau after breaking down his gate, as well as many offline threats and conspiracies to commit violence (Beckett, 2020). In addition, many known QAnon activists participated in the deadly January 2021 siege of the U.S. Capitol (Daly, 2021). Recognizing in the aftermath that much of that action had been planned and coordinated on social media, Twitter and other mainstream platforms implemented sweeping bans on QAnon content and supporters (*Associated Press*, 2021). This move, of course, likely only drove the content and supporters further into the dark web, where such coordinated action can continue in secret.

Threats and incitements of violence occur frequently on sites like 4chan (Nickey, 2015) and appear to be one of the expectations of regular use. Indeed, a scholarly study of deep web social media site traffic and posts (Malevich and Robertson, 2020) concluded that "these sites often act as a self-reinforcing community of users encouraging each other to violence." Also common—and often accompanied by threats of violence—are posts that reveal personal information about celebrities, journalists, and other public figures in a practice called *doxxing*, as well as the release of celebrity photographs, videos, and even fabricated images.

Doxxing attacks are typically related to social or political issues associated with the target(s). For example, an entertainer may be doxxed after being vocal about supporting a feminist cause or joking about abortion policy; a politician may be doxxed after supporting—or not supporting—a bill; and a journalist may be doxxed after writing about a controversial topic or event. The act of releasing someone's personal information in a public forum carries an implied threat on its own, but the (usually anonymous) doxxer also often encourages or at least suggests specific acts of violence to be carried out. Typically, the first sign of being doxxed is the sudden receipt of numerous unwanted and abusive phone calls and text messages from unknown and/or blocked numbers. According to research by the Reporters Committee for Freedom of the Press (Henrichsen, 2015): "These can range from relatively benign messages to rape and death threats."

One of the best-known examples is the mass doxxing and harassment of women in the gaming industry known as "Gamergate." It all seemed to begin when independent game designer Zoe Quinn released a new game called "Depression Quest" in 2013, though the vitriol surrounding women in gaming had been brewing for much longer on dark web sites. The game's release was merely the tipping point at which the anonymous anger rising in the darkness of 8chan spilled out into the light of mainstream society. Quinn was an early target in a massive campaign of harassment that soon included game developer Brianna Wu, media critic Anita Sarkeesian, and seemingly every feminist writer who dared to comment on the controversy.

After their phone numbers, addresses, pictures, and more were shared publicly, the targets received thousands of calls and messages, had their social media accounts hacked, and were forced from their homes on multiple occasions after receiving credible threats that promised—in graphic detail—severe beatings, sexual assault, and murder. Some of the threats also targeted friends and family members. The harassment escalated to such an extent that some of the victims altered their appearances, changed their names, and avoided being seen in public; others left the gaming industry entirely. For those who refused to give in to the anonymous attackers, the abuse continued for years and completely altered their lives. Quinn gave up hope that it would ever stop, explaining in a 2015 interview: "Even if you vanish, or even if you stick around, no matter what, nothing changes. These [anonymous attackers] never stop. So, all right, accept that as a given. And then it's like, who I was before all this, she's dead. That life is over. That's just a fact" (Machkovech, 2015).

In 2016, a journalist who now writes using a pseudonym had her personal information posted on a series of Craigslist advertisements, some offering sex for money and others claiming she had "a rape fantasy" and wanted to be tied up and sexually assaulted. The latter ads included the chilling instruction "Don't take no for an answer." For months, she received countless threatening and abusive phone calls, text messages, and social media posts (some with lewd and degrading images) from people she didn't know, who were responding to ads posted by someone else she didn't know—and was never able to identify. In a piece published about her experience the following year (Scheffler, 2017), she wrote:

> I still shudder every time I think of the fact that someone is out there waiting for me to let my guard down … [E]very time I publish something new, there's a part of me that wonders if this will be the day the verbal threats become physical—if this will be the day I really am silenced.

In some cases, a doxxing victim may receive unwanted deliveries at their home or work. Although the items are often rather innocuous—like a pizza with an unappetizing combination of toppings—they clearly reveal that the anonymous sender knows the physical location of the victim's residence or workplace. The type of doxxing known as *swatting* is particularly dangerous and frightening. It involves an anonymous perpetrator calling the police to report an active shooter or armed hostage situation at the victim's location, with the hope that a SWAT team will arrive, break down the victim's door, and arrest them. In 2014, gamer Jordan Mathewson, known online by the moniker "Kootra," was a victim of swatting while conducting a live stream from his office, so the frightening experience was captured on video. Mathewson later said that he was "terrified" during the incident (Padilla, 2014), in which he was ordered to the ground at gunpoint while the entire office was searched by heavily armed officers.

What makes campaigns of anonymous abuse and harassment even more frustrating is that there is often very little recourse for the victims, particularly if the actions remain only online. Many women who work in the media have written and spoken about their personal experiences with being doxxed, receiving threats via all forms of media, having their social media and email accounts hacked, and being stalked online. Virtually all of them say that they received very little or no help from law enforcement. The excuses vary—police cannot identify the culprits, they haven't technically violated a law, or the evidence is too weak—but the outcome is the same: the victims are on their own.

Journalist Amanda Hess suggests that the pool of targets for online harassment is far larger than many people may believe. After offering just a few examples of the vile, menacing messages she has received throughout her career, Hess (2014) wrote: "None of this makes me exceptional. It just makes me a woman with an internet connection." She and journalist Anna Merlan (2015) have each written about being essentially dismissed by police when they reported online harassment—and how common this is for their female colleagues—as well as feeling frustrated while trying to explain the realm of social media to members of law enforcement. Hess reported that the police officer who took her statement about receiving rape and death threats on social media, in all seriousness, asked her: "What is Twitter?"

## Positioning powerless perpetrators

Many people who are active on dark web social media consider themselves to be social outcasts and help to foster a sense of community for one another. As part of what has been dubbed their "outcast culture" (Nickey, 2015), dark web social media posts frequently include unflattering references to "normal" people in society, often expressed using the term "normie." Their activities can be understood as a way of striking back from a powerless position against mainstream society and the people who are celebrated within it. They can effectively seize some of their victim's personal and/or physical power by inciting violence against them or by making believable threats that result in limiting the celebrity's movements and consuming their thoughts. Further, hacking the personal technology and accounts of celebrities, as well as publicly releasing personal information about them, can lead to financial harm, identity theft, and other losses of economic power.

The nefarious activities carried out on the dark web are supported by its fundamental feature of anonymity. A covert attacker can enjoy the fallout of their actions under the cover of darkness and without fear of reprisal. They won't receive any official credit, of course, but they can anonymously claim the misdeed in their dark web community and secretly enjoy the fallout, which would likely be heavily publicized in mainstream media and publicly debated.

Even in the absence of an online community, covert attackers may experience enough personal satisfaction for the act alone to be worthwhile. For example, long before Tor and 4chan existed, there was the "Max Headroom incident." Max Headroom was a fictional character on British television in the 1980s that was purported to be the product of artificial intelligence and was quite well known at the time, even appearing in a U.S. commercial for Coca-Cola. One evening in November 1987, two Chicago television stations were briefly hijacked in separate incidents two hours apart, apparently by the same anonymous hacker(s). First was WGN-TV during the 9pm newscast for 28 seconds, and then PBS affiliate WTTW's broadcast of *Doctor Who* was interrupted for 90 seconds. In each incident, the program was replaced by a video of a person wearing a Max Headroom mask and costume, along with distorted audio and, in the second video, bizarre behavior that included the person exposing their buttocks while someone else spanked them with a flyswatter. After that, the feed returned to regular programming. Although most people would not describe the Max Headroom incident as violent, it was certainly disturbing—and the total nonsense of its content could easily be viewed as potentially threatening.

The Max Headroom prankster(s) never repeated the act for a third time or came out of hiding to claim credit. And now, some 30 years later, they have also never been caught. The incident itself generated an abundance of public attention, and numerous theories were developed and debated. One of the most popular was that the culprit(s) were current or former employees of one or both TV stations looking for a way to strike back against perceived company wrongdoing. This seems plausible, especially considering the power differential between the employee-perpetrators and the employer-target, as well as the apparent senselessness of the act. Whether true or not, the perpetrator(s) certainly gained plenty of self-satisfaction (that is, personal power) after pulling off what has been called "television's most infamous hack" (Haskins, 2017).

Perhaps the latest nightmare for celebrities and public figures in the digital age are *deepfakes*, also known as *deepfake videos*. A combination of "fake" and "deep learning" (a machine learning method that employs techniques of artificial intelligence), the technology allows for near-seamless replacement of one person in an existing video or image with the likeness of someone else. Although image modification and replacement are far from new concepts—the techniques have been used in film production and political campaigns for decades—what makes the practice novel now is the ease with which almost anyone can produce and distribute them. Moreover, the relevant technologies have become so sophisticated in recent years that distinguishing a deepfake from a real video is becoming virtually impossible (O'Brien, 2019).

Many deepfakes are created mostly for fun and cause negligible harm. More than one film star has had their face replaced with that of someone much older, much younger, a different color, or a different gender in one of these fake videos. In addition to looking somewhat creepy, the videos that seem intended just for laughs are usually also obviously phony. Some of the more disturbing—and potentially damaging—versions include pornographic films that feature celebrities who, without their consent, have been substituted for the actual actors. In fact, visual threat intelligence company Sensity reported in 2019 that nonconsensual deepfake pornography accounts for 96 percent of all deepfake videos online (Patrini, 2019).

Other deepfakes purport to show high-profile people, especially politicians, committing crimes or engaged in other unseemly behavior. An emerging area of concern involves "synthetic voice audio and images of nonexistent, synthetic people" that have been used to destabilize political processes and damage businesses worldwide (Patrini, 2019). All that is needed to create a deepfake is a high-quality video and a high-quality image of the person who will substitute for the real actor. Distribution is just a matter of posting the video via a mainstream social media platform (for example, YouTube or Instagram), an outlet on the dark web, or an anonymous social networking app.

Perhaps the most famous of those anonymous apps is Yik Yak, which was available for iOS and Android from 2013 to 2017 and quickly earned a reputation for its widespread use for cyberbullying and espousing hate speech (Franklin, 2021). Like other location-specific apps, Yik Yak allowed users to share and view posts (called "yaks") only with others within a five-mile radius. Although many yaks were innocuous or even positive, the threat of the menacing ones was only enhanced by the app's requirements of physical proximity and anonymity. In December 2015, for example, dozens of profanity-laced posts that threatened students of color at Western Washington University appeared on anonymous, location-specific platforms, including a yak reading "let's lynch her" that was directed at a Black student leader and eventually found to have been posted by a white male student at the University (Hutton, 2017).

In 2021, Yik Yak was relaunched for iOS with new owners who promised both "the same Yik Yak experience millions knew and loved" and "a fun place free of bullying, threats, and all sorts of negativity" (Franklin, 2021). The current version of the app requires that users agree to refrain from bullying, abusive, and threatening behaviors, or else risk being banned from the platform. However, anonymity and physical proximity remain hallmarks of Yik Yak, and new causes for concern have arisen since the relaunch. In May 2022, user David Teather published a blog post explaining how Yik Yak functionality places users at risk for being identified, stalked, or otherwise monitored without their knowledge. In the post, Teather (2022) wrote that he "was able to access the precise GPS coordinates (accurate to within 10–15ft) of all posts and comments on the YikYak platform," going on to explain that cross-referencing that information with users' Yik Yak handles makes it "possible to de-anonymize users." Yik Yak has since released an updated version of the app that no longer exposes the problematic personal information, but the company did not simultaneously disable that functionality in previous app versions, which remain available for use (Sato, 2022).

Dozens of similar apps were developed during Yik Yak's four-year hiatus, and more are likely to come. For example, the app *DASH* claims to allow for anonymous, location-based chats that are never saved on the company server or possible to capture with a screenshot by others. Most of the companies behind these apps, however, are technically capable of identifying users— even if just by IP address—but vow not to do so without their consent or a verified warrant from law enforcement.

It is important to note that the handful of people who have been identified and/or arrested for crimes like hacking, doxxing, and inciting or plotting violent acts on the dark web tend to be among those who also engage in *overt* violence. Thus, they appear to represent a tiny fraction of the thousands of people involved in planning, coordinating, and encouraging such violence in secret. Those covert perpetrators are far more difficult to catch. As technology continues to advance, especially in the areas of automation and artificial intelligence, their digital disguises may only improve. This means it could become easier for perpetrators to commit acts of covert violence— perhaps without ever having to expose themselves—and simultaneously more difficult to apprehend them.

## References

*Associated Press*. (2021, January 12). Social media crackdown continues after siege of US Capitol. https://apnews.com/article/election-2020-conspir acy-theories-media-inaugurations-elections-b9bce4774cee905d22508 93cfec6bf6f

Beckett, L. (2020, October 16). QAnon: A timeline of violence linked to the conspiracy. *The Guardian*. https://www.theguardian.com/us-news/ 2020/oct/15/qanon-violence-crimes-timeline

Daly, K. (2021, January 7). The Capitol siege's QAnon roots. *Axios*. https://www.axios.com/capitol-sieges-qanon-roots-acadc659-4d39-4606-96c3-a477c6841fe3.html

Franklin, J. (2021, August 17). Yik Yak, the anonymous app that tested free speech, is back. *NPR*. https://www.npr.org/2021/08/17/1028402237/yik-yak-anonymous-app-free-speech-returns

Haskins, C. (2017, November 22). Television's most infamous hack is still a mystery 30 years later. *Vice*. https://www.vice.com/en/article/59yvj5/max-headroom-hack-anniversary

Henrichsen, J. (2015, May 19). The dangers of journalism include getting doxed: Here's what you can do about it. *Poynter*. https://www.poynter.org/reporting-editing/2015/the-dangers-of-journalism-include-getting-doxxed-heres-what-you-can-do-about-it/

Hess, A. (2014, January 6). Why women aren't welcome on the internet. *Pacific Standard*. https://psmag.com/social-justice/women-arent-welcome-internet-72170

Hessler, C., Jr. (2020, June 3). Man who stalked local TV news anchor sent to jail. *Delaware County Daily Times*. https://www.delcotimes.com/news/man-who-stalked-local-tv-news-anchor-sent-to-jail/article_edc7a3aa-c328-5514-ba67-dfda01501075.html

Hutton, C. (2017, January 12). WWU student gets probation for posting "lynch her" about Black student body president. *Bellingham Herald*. https://www.bellinghamherald.com/news/local/crime/article126227029.html

Machkovech, S. (2015, March 25). "That life is over": Zoe Quinn looks beyond GamerGate. *Ars Technica*. https://arstechnica.com/gaming/2015/03/that-life-is-over-zoe-quinn-looks-beyond-gamergate/

Malevich, S., and Robertson, T. (2020). Violence begetting violence: An examination of extremist content on deep web social networks. *First Monday, 25*(3). https://doi.org/10.5210/fm.v25i3.10421

Merlan, A. (2015, January 29). The cops don't care about violent online threats. What do we do now? *Jezebel*. https://jezebel.com/the-cops-dont-care-about-violent-online-threats-what-d-1682577343

Nickey, L.N. (2015, October 6). How 4chan has become connected to threats of violence. *Daily Pennsylvanian*. https://www.thedp.com/article/2015/10/4chan-and-connection-to-violence-threats

O'Brien, M. (2019, June 12). Why "deepfake" videos are becoming more difficult to detect. *PBS News Hour*. https://www.pbs.org/newshour/show/why-deepfake-videos-are-becoming-more-difficult-to-detect

Padilla, A. (2014, August 28). Gamer Kootra "swatted" while livestreaming: Jordan Mathewson talks about how he reacted in the video. *ABS News—Tampa Bay*. https://www.abcactionnews.com/news/local-news/gamer-kootra-swatted-while-livestreaming-jordan-mathewson-talks-about-how-he-reacted-in-the-video

Patrini, G. (2019, July 10). Mapping the deepfake landscape. *Sensity*. https://sensity.ai/mapping-the-deepfake-landscape/

Sato, M. (2022, May 13). Anonymous bulletin board app Yik Yak is revealing its users' exact locations. *The Verge*. https://www.theverge.com/2022/5/13/23070696/yik-yak-anonymous-app-precise-locations-revealed

Scheffler, R. (2017, July 13). I got doxxed by a stranger—and the online harassment quickly took over my life. *Vox*. https://www.vox.com/first-person/2017/7/13/15960394/online-sexual-harassment-doxxing-craigslist

Teather, D. (2022, May 9). YikYak is exposing millions of user locations. *The Response Times*. https://theresponsetimes.com/yikyak-is-exposing-user-locations/

Wendling, M. (2021, January 7). QAnon: What is it and where did it come from? *BBC News*. https://www.bbc.com/news/53498434

Wilson, S., Dempsey, C., Farnham, F., Manze, T., and Taylor, A. (2018). Stalking risks to celebrities and public figures. *BJPsych Advances, 24*, 152–160. https://www.cambridge.org/core/journals/bjpsych-advances/article/stalking-risks-to-celebrities-and-public-figures/B389AB3D8AC6A3641C8320C8D2BABB07

Wise, J. (2010, October 8). Most likely to be stalked: Why female news anchors are more likely to be pursued by delusional men. *Psychology Today*. https://www.psychologytoday.com/us/blog/extreme-fear/201010/most-likely-be-stalked

8

# Shining Light on the Shadows

Preventing covert violence is perhaps even more difficult than preventing overt forms of criminal behavior. To a large degree, this is because the covert version is often harder to detect and/or is easily misunderstood as something else. Enough cases of presumed accidental deaths subsequently turn out to be murders that we can reasonably assume that many acts of covert violence are either never discovered or never identified as intentional.

Some incidents remain in an indefinite state of uncertainty within the minds of officials. The Pepsi and Tylenol cases in Chapter 4 are perfect examples, as each implicates customers and companies in plots that they may or may not have initiated. Similarly, the 2001 anthrax attacks in the aftermath of 9/11 continue to generate significantly divided opinions among experts and members of the public as to their origins, with some accusing prominent scientists or the 9/11 terrorists and others promoting conspiracy theories that involve images of a deep state within the U.S. federal government. If those infamous incidents were never officially solved, then it would not be surprising to find that many lower-profile cases are missed entirely.

Unlike unsolved cases, in which the action is recognized as malicious even if the identity of the perpetrator is unknown or ambiguous, undetected covert cases produce nothing that appears to need solving. Compared to maliciously inflicted injuries and deaths, those that are deemed accidental, due to natural causes, or self-inflicted generally require much less (if any) investigation and follow-up. And once an official classification has been made, there are virtually no mechanisms in place for routine reconsideration. It often takes years of persistence from a victim's friend or family member to convince an authority figure to take another look, and frequently that suspicious person must uncover some kind of new evidence before they find anyone who will listen.

There are also practical reasons for not investigating a death when the manner and/or cause appears to be obvious. Determining the exact cause of a death requires available and sufficient funding, as well as other limited resources such as the time and expertise of physicians and/or other scientists.

The autopsy process typically begins with a thorough visual exam of the entire body; after that, every organ is removed and weighed, and samples are taken from organs, fluids, and tissues for further testing and examination. If this typical process fails to produce a definitive answer, very few jurisdictions have sufficient resources available for advanced testing (Khurshid et al., 2022). It would be impractical to follow this protocol for every human death and, therefore, autopsies primarily are reserved for deaths that appear suspicious or were unexpected. (Autopsies are also commonly performed in the event of a public health concern, when requested by a deceased person's doctor or family member, and when compelled by a court of law.) In some cases, family members might refuse an autopsy for their deceased loved one, even when important evidence could be discovered. Religious and/or cultural tenets may forbid the procedure, and a longstanding conflict between science and religion continues to fuel distrust in medicine and forensics among groups of people worldwide, particularly those with low levels of education (Khurshid et al., 2022).

Moreover, the U.S. legal standard required for a criminal conviction—guilt beyond a reasonable doubt—is a high bar to achieve. If there is not enough evidence present, perhaps it is easier or more practical to classify a possible homicide as something else. Plus, with law enforcement jurisdictions across the United States under pressure to reduce murder rates and close current homicide cases as quickly as possible, it might be tempting to ignore a nagging suspicion or avoid digging too deeply into a complicated injury or death.

Despite these and other difficulties, there are strategies that hold promise for reducing the incidence of covert violence. This chapter describes three of those strategies, which can be substantiated with ample data and examples, but are seldom used for the purpose at hand. Although the focus here is on the U.S. context, these strategies could be applied to help address covert violence in other nations with similar economic, social, and/or cultural circumstances.

## Addressing power in society

First, *the appeal and operation of power must be addressed.* This means finding more effective and safer outlets for members of society who feel powerless and marginalized or experience shame and mistrust; reducing the entitlements of high-status groups that, once denied, often lead to frustration, anger, and violence; and increasing the credibility of conventional solutions for difficult personal and political issues.

### The pain of powerlessness

Many Americans today feel profoundly deprived in an economic sense. Income inequality in the United States is the worst among the nations that comprise the intergovernmental organization known as the Group of Seven (G7), which also includes Canada, France, Germany, Italy, Japan, and the United Kingdom (Schaeffer, 2020). Over the past 50 years, the gap between the rich and the average American has steadily increased, and it's becoming increasingly difficult to distinguish the middle class from the poor. By 2018, the highest-earning 20 percent of U.S. households (making $130,001 or more that year) accounted for 52 percent of the country's total income, with nearly half of that—almost one quarter of all U.S. income that year—going just to the highest-earning 5 percent of households (Schaeffer, 2020). This means that 80 percent of Americans now share *less than half* of the country's total income. In contrast, the same top-earning tier of U.S. households earned 43 percent of all income in 1968, leaving 57 percent to share among the bottom 80 percent of American households.

A similar pattern is found in the distribution of wealth in the United States, with obvious links to the Great Recession of 2007–2009. Median family wealth plummeted from a high of $146,600 in 2006 to just $87,800 in 2013 (all amounts are in 2018 dollars; see Horowitz et al., 2020). The recovery since then has been slow overall, with median family wealth rising to just $101,800 by 2016. That figure, however, tends to mask the fact that wealth increases since 2007 have exclusively gone to the highest-earning U.S. families, who now hold about 80 percent of the country's total wealth. With just 20 percent of the nation's wealth shared among the lower four fifths of the population, it should be little surprise that the median wealth of the lowest-earning 20 percent of U.S. households has consistently been either zero or negative in recent decades (Horowitz et al., 2020).

Increasing economic inequality breeds additional social insecurities and despair. According to a Pew Research Center poll from December 2018 (Parker et al., 2019), U.S. adults are generally pessimistic about the future of the nation. Nearly three quarters say that the gap between the rich and poor will likely increase over the next 30 years, and two thirds think that political divisions will worsen. Nearly half say they are "very worried" that U.S. leaders will be able to solve the country's biggest problems, with only 12 percent saying that they are "not too" or "not at all" worried. Moreover, respondents expressed little faith that Social Security benefits will be available by the time they retire, as well as increased worry about more jobs being replaced by automation.

The global COVID-19 pandemic that began in January 2020 only made matters worse. In the United States, small-business revenue plummeted, and temporary shutdowns and layoffs increasingly turned into permanent ones as the months went by (Bauer et al., 2020). Millions of people who wanted to work were forced out of the labor market, and more than one fifth of households in at least 26 U.S. states were behind on their rent by July (Bauer et al., 2020). Food insecurity surged above Great Recession peaks, especially among households with children, as widespread school closures limited access to free and reduced-price meals for many students, and also contributed to parents leaving the labor force (Bauer et al., 2020). Simultaneously, feelings of loneliness and social exclusion increased as people quarantined at home and dramatically decreased social interactions and community engagement over long stretches of time. By June 2020, the Centers for Disease Control and Prevention reported "considerably elevated adverse mental health conditions associated with COVID-19" among Americans, including increased substance use and elevated suicidal ideation (Czeisler et al., 2020). These stresses and their consequences were found to be even worse for those in vulnerable populations, such as older adults (Robb et al., 2020) and those who already suffered with mental health and/or substance use disorders before the pandemic (Panchal et al., 2020). Increased levels of inflation have exacerbated the pain and suffering of the average citizen.

These trends paint a picture of hardship among Americans that has steadily grown worse in recent decades, and the resulting suffering is evident in U.S. adults' social views and expectations for the future. Indeed, a majority of U.S. adults agree that there is too much economic inequality in the nation (Horowitz et al., 2020) and that increasing government spending on education and affordable healthcare for all would improve the quality of life for future generations of Americans (Parker et al., 2019). If nothing is done to improve the economic situation for so many Americans—and to reverse the pattern of the rich becoming richer to the detriment of everyone else—then the already-evident patterns toward greater political polarization (Dimock and Wike, 2020), online harassment and abuse (Vogels, 2021), social isolation (McPherson et al., 2006), and other societal ills surely will continue to rise.

Profound economic hardship by itself can trigger frustration and anger, but add to that the promised rewards of the so-called "American dream" and the entitlements of American exceptionalism, and the result can be an especially toxic brand of resentment. People who are accustomed to being treated fairly and with respect will understandably come to feel entitled to a continuation of their advantaged position, and in the United States, that especially pertains to boys and men, white people, and straight/heterosexual people. It's no coincidence that these are the same groups that have long been more prone to violence than others. In addition, the combination of 85 percent of Americans who say that the United States is one of the greatest countries in the world (Geiger, 2018) and the 60 percent who say that it will become less important on the world stage (Parker et al., 2019) seems like a breeding ground for future hostility.

## Credibility of conventions

The lack of faith and confidence in American leadership is in part a result of the growing presence of economic hardship. But the source of U.S. leaders' disrepute goes beyond their failure to create a more equitable distribution of income and assets. The results of a 2020 Gallup poll (Brenan, 2020) make the credibility of most U.S. leaders from a broad range of spheres and disciplines appear to be at the level of the stereotypical used car sales force. According to Gallup, only 6 percent of U.S. adults voiced a great deal of confidence in Congress, just 10 percent in the criminal justice system, and 22 percent in the presidency. Outside of government, other social institutions fared only slightly better. When asked to evaluate the honesty and ethical standards of various occupational groups, less than 20 percent of the respondents gave very high marks to lawyers, bankers, business executives, journalists, nursing home operators, advertising practitioners, or even clergy.

Efforts to prevent acts of terrorism present us with a model that can be modified to fit many social, educational, economic, and personal issues as well. Somehow, we must reinstate the credibility of our public officials so that alienated and powerless Americans do not feel the need to go outside of mainstream conventions and radicalize their behavior in order to satisfy their goals. Bringing Americans back into the mainstream may be the most effective long-term strategy for preventing future incidents of social and political violence. Everyone benefits when others in society trust the social institutions that are in place to resolve disputes and personal problems, and do not feel the need to go to the margins of society—to secret acts of covert violence—for such solutions. In the same way, bosses, teachers and school administrators, physicians, police officers, and parents—indeed, anyone in charge of other people—must be able to garner the respect and confidence of those over whom they exercise authority and control. This, of course, is far easier said than done. But unless authority—in other words, power that is generally accepted as legitimate—becomes widespread, social problems will fester under the surface of society.

In the workplace, a reduction in covert violence may require company managers to take a more humane approach to their employees' status on the job (Fox and Levin, 1994). The immediate situation in which a worker is fired tends to be the most dangerous and threatening time period for company supervisors and bosses. Rather than attempting to distance company personnel from a terminated worker, human resources might just take the opposite approach and *immediately* engage in aggressive outplacement counseling. Many former workers should be allowed to come back to the worksite; their termination should occur when they are able to be in touch with their supervisors, and not over a weekend when they are left entirely alone to deal with their misfortune.

Unless an employee is terminated for cause, company representatives should make a serious and swift effort to help the ex-worker find another job. During the rash of workplace violence from vengeful ex-workers in the 1990s, frightened bosses around the country began to hire companies that specialize in assisting fired workers to find decent alternative employment in a timely fashion. As the workplace murder rate declined over the years and the credibility of management increased, the presumed viability of such specialized companies finally subsided. Both overt and covert manifestations of violence dissipated as a result.

## Greater social awareness

Second, *social awareness, or mindfulness, should be given greater emphasis.* For one thing, even when red flags are present, social norms related to politeness and expectations of privacy may prevent bystanders from intervening in dangerous situations and/or in the lives of threatening individuals when they otherwise could do so.

A culture of silence is learned from an early age. Parents teach their children that it is "not nice to tattle." As a result, many decent individuals grow into adulthood believing that it is morally wrong to inform on a family member, a fellow student, or a friend. Moreover, in prisons, those who "snitch" or "rat" on a fellow inmate assume a position at the bottom of the status hierarchy. Yet, in contemporary urban settings, the culture of silence may result from more than a desire for social acceptance; there is reason to believe that fear of retaliation, in a physical sense, may also play a role. Eyewitnesses are often reluctant to share information with law enforcement, fearing that they will be placed in harm's way, and many others simply do not trust the police.

Similarly, there are many students who were unwilling to "snitch" on their peers during the string of rampage shootings that have plagued schools across the United States. Some students refused to cooperate, even when they overheard threats being discussed in their high school corridors by disgruntled and angry classmates. Then, following an effective campaign to secure the cooperation of students, the culture of silence was all but broken. Many schools implemented bystander prevention programs, including anonymous email systems and telephone hotlines to counteract the hesitancy to inform on peers and encourage students to be more active about reporting troublesome behavior (Madfis, 2020). Importantly, designated members of the school staff became available as trusted depositories of information about threatening student conversations—with remarkably positive results.

Moreover, the April 1999 Columbine school massacre of 12 students and one teacher in Littleton, Colorado, convinced numerous high school students across the country to take their troublesome schoolmates more seriously. More often than before that tragedy, youngsters who overheard threatening conversations in the hallway or who knew the identity of worrisome students were willing to communicate that information to a resource officer, a teacher, or a parent. In the Boston area, for example, students at a suburban high school may have averted disaster when they informed a resource officer about a Columbine-style plan to "shoot up" the school. In southern New Jersey, a

15-year-old girl informed the school's principal about a similar conspiracy, thereby thwarting a deadly plot against students and teachers on a hit list.

However, factors responsible for reducing school rampage shootings may not be generalizable to everyday acts of student violence. The fact that so many students have tried to poison their teachers while school was in session and classmates were in attendance suggests an important possibility—namely, that many people believe that their peers will simply not break the social prohibitions against snitching that pervade numerous communities, no matter how damaging or deadly the illegal acts may be. Further, the uncertainty of covert acts of violence may make it even more difficult for bystanders to stop—or even to identify—them. Inserting an unknown substance into a teacher's water bottle, for example, may seem vastly more ambiguous as a threat to life than a student threatening to bring a loaded gun to school, and therefore less demanding of intervention.

The importance of social awareness goes far beyond the relationship between students and teachers. Some covert killers have escaped detection until being identified by an associate or family member. After remaining on the loose for 18 years, having committed three murders and 16 bombings, the so-called Unabomber was finally brought to justice in 1995, thanks to the intervention of a concerned member of his family. Reading the 33,000-word manifesto—an anti-technology essay published, as he demanded, in the *Washington Post*—David Kaczinski recognized his fugitive brother's prose style and submitted a tip to the FBI.

As clichéd as it has become, the importance of "see something, say something" really can make a big difference when it comes to averting covert violence. In so many cases, bystanders in retrospect have remembered sensing at the time that something was "off" or "just didn't seem right," but disregarded the feeling, often out of a desire not to disrupt a social situation or violate social norms. However, trusting one's "gut" is frequently reliable, and merely mentioning a bad feeling to a proper authority can make an enormous difference—perhaps even the difference between life and death. We, as a society, must reduce the costs of coming forward in ambiguous situations and increase the incentives for doing so.

The social awareness of covert killing apparently never made its way into totally effective forms of international law. Military uses of covert violence might be substantially limited by an internationally applied legal remedy that includes adequate enforcement provisions for the use, storage, and testing of biological and chemical weapons. In 1925, the Geneva Protocol, a treaty that prohibited the use of chemical and biological weapons in international armed conflicts, banned germ warfare. The Protocol was signed by 108 nations, but unfortunately failed to include any method for verifying and sanctioning noncompliance. The Protocol also did not ban the development, production, or stockpiling of such weaponry. It was later supplemented by the Biological Weapons Convention (BWC) which as of August 2019 committed its 183 state signatories to prohibit the development, production, and stockpiling of biological and toxin weapons. However, not unlike its 1925 predecessor, the BWC failed to include any formal verification regime for monitoring compliance.

In the American experience, awareness of the battered person syndrome has somewhat improved the condition of marital relations and divorce over the last few decades. Likewise, services available to the victims of domestic abuse have reduced the number of husbands murdered by their wives and parents by their (adult) children. Battered family members now have clearer alternatives to killing their abusers—in either an overt or covert manner—including restraining orders, help with relocating to safe accommodations, and, at the very least, more confidence in counting on law enforcement and courts to take seriously their victimization. The intimacy of family relations contributes a good deal to enhancing areas of disagreement and conflict. Linda Lusk, chief advancement officer for the Center for Abuse and Rape Emergencies (CARE), said orders of protection, also known as restraining orders, "have doubled during the pandemic"—a time when many couples and families were holed up at home and isolated from friends and work.

## Prioritizing covert cases

Third, *members of society, including the FBI, should prioritize the reduction of more nuanced or passive methods of human destruction—including poisonings, drug overdoses, drownings, arson, and explosives—alongside the more sensational methods such as firearms and knives.* This especially means distributing greater resources for investigative procedures and techniques for detecting the presence of dangerous substances at the time of death.

Shootings and stabbings are rarely employed surreptitiously. Their perpetrators usually operate out in the open. In the aftermath, they might commit suicide, engage in combat with law enforcement, or attempt to escape. Their modus operandi is entirely obvious and visible. In fact, those killers who look for celebrity status hope to attract as much publicity as possible.

Among the range of covert methods for taking the life of a victim, poison seems to be among the most difficult for the authorities to identify. This might help to explain why so few cases of fatal poisoning are found in FBI annual reports, despite the comparatively large numbers of apparently accidental and intentionally self-inflicted deadly poisonings. Yet, the expenses and personnel required to perform routine toxicology procedures for the detection of poisonous substances may be unavailable to local homicide investigators and medical examiners. Moreover, exotic poisons do not always leave telltale clues that hint at their presence. In most cases, homicide detectives and medical personnel appear likely to accept the obvious if incorrect conclusion—that a death was a result of a sudden illness such as a heart attack or of a long-term ailment of an unexplained origin. The possibility of poisoning seems to be the last of their considerations for determining whether (and how) a death has occurred.

Similarly, a fatal fall in the victim's home can be easily regarded as accidental rather than a result of shoving someone down a flight of stairs. A nursing home patient who suddenly stops breathing is likely to be regarded as a casualty of old age rather than a victim of smothering by a member of the staff. A swimmer who drowns during a family vacation may be viewed as succumbing to a rough undertow rather than being held under water by a companion.

Just like members of the public, when homicide investigators think of murder, they are most likely to conjure up sensationalized images of gang warfare, school rampages, family stabbings, or mass shooters. Passive-aggressive and clandestine alternatives such as poisoning, pushing and shoving, smothering, drowning, and fire-starting may be totally ignored. It is not surprising, then, that so few episodes of covert murder ever make their way into annual FBI homicide reports.

When shootings or stabbings are not involved, the deaths of elderly individuals are especially likely to be regarded officially as a result of natural causes. In the absence of substantiating evidence, older men and women who die by means of poisoning, suffocation, or strangulation are too often regarded as victims of old age rather than criminal mischief. That is what happened in the 1988 deaths of sisters Cordelia and Girlie Norton, of Llano, Texas, and Olgie Nobles, of San Angelo, who were all assumed to have died by natural means, despite sharing highly unusual circumstances (see Chapter 2). Yet, toxicology tests are rarely conducted, and few autopsies take place. Police investigators decline to ask in-depth questions regarding the elderly victim's finances or relationships. Bodies are sent to funeral homes for burial or cremation before a physician has been given a chance to check for signs of foul play. Clues about potential motives for murder—the family members who have been overburdened with caretaker responsibilities, the "good Samaritans" who recently befriended a lonely victim, or a sudden surge in deaths in the ward of a nursing home—are frequently overlooked.

In Vermillion County, Indiana, the 1995 death of 69-year-old Robert Biddle was treated as if the retired custodian had expired from heart trouble, even though just a few weeks before his passing, two women whom Biddle had met at a local diner moved into his residence. Biddle's original cause of death seemed quite routine, so a medical examiner never examined the body and police dismissed reports that the victim had been fearful of his new pair of roommates. Seven months passed before Biddle's body was exhumed and an autopsy finally revealed the actual reason for his demise: smothering, presumably with a pillow by one of his housemates while he slept in his bed. Apparently, his newfound friends were hoping to collect on his inheritance.

Covert killing of elderly victims may be far more common than ever suspected by most medical examiners and investigators (Levine, 2000). At the same time, some police departments have established specialized units to investigate elder assaults and deaths. In addition, hospitals are creating elder death review teams consisting of social workers, physicians, police, lawyers, and members of protective services. Some states require that every nursing home death be reported to the medical examiner's office. Police officers in some jurisdictions have been trained to investigate important factors at the crime scene involving an elderly person's death, rather than immediately assuming natural causes. These are positive trends that should continue; hopefully more detectives are taught to initiate death investigations by first ruling out the possibility of homicide.

## A final cautionary note

It should now be clear that many homicides go undetected each year in the United States—especially those involving poisoning, arson, drowning, crushing, or falling—and, thus, that many killers unjustly go free. Yet, in the process of investing more resources into investigating harmful incidents that are more nuanced, less histrionic, and perhaps more difficult to solve (or prove), law enforcement and prosecutorial teams must be careful not to move too far in the opposite direction; in other words, convicting someone for a murder that never occurred (that is, an accidental, natural, or self-inflicted death that is misclassified as a homicide) is also terribly unjust.

Criminal convictions of innocent people are certainly rare, but they do occur. And some of those cases are eventually overturned. The National Registry of Exonerations (2021) has counted a total of 2,795 exonerations in the United States from 1989 to June 1, 2021. These instances—perhaps just a fraction of all U.S. wrongful convictions, many of which lack the evidence and/or advocacy needed to prove actual innocence—include more than 15,000 years of prison time served by people who were wrongly convicted of murder. Although comprehensive data on worldwide exonerations are difficult to find, Amnesty International (2022) tracks the number of exonerated people who had been sentenced to death, reporting seven such cases across four countries in 2021 (one each in Bahrain and Kenya, two in the U.S., and three in Zambia).

Just imagine waking up in the home you share with your ailing parents, for whom you provide care, because your father is yelling for help and saying something about a fire. You race to the living room and see that the couch is in flames, which your mother is frantically trying to extinguish with a towel. You run to the kitchen, fill a pitcher with water, return to the living room, throw the water on the blaze, and then watch in dismay as the fire only gets worse. Fearing real danger now, you yell for your parents to escape out the back door while you call 911. As the fire grows rapidly, you make the call and then flee out the front door. When emergency responders arrive, you direct them to the backyard, where your parents should be waiting. Suddenly there's an explosion and the sound of glass shattering. The house is fully engulfed now. Then, to your horror, first responders tell you that your parents did not, in fact, make it out on their own and had to be pulled out. But it's too late, and both subsequently succumb to their injuries. Later, investigators conclude with certainty that the fire had been deliberately started and then promptly announce the arrest of their prime suspect: *you*.

That is what happened to 31-year-old Paul Camiolo, the only child of Edward and Rosalie Camiolo, of Upper Moreland, Pennsylvania. His nightmare began one early morning in September 1996, when the fire started—likely by accident related to his mother's smoking—and continued for years as he was accused of deliberately setting it to kill his parents and collect the proceeds from their life insurance. Fire investigators found evidence of gasoline on the living room floor under the carpet, and they doubted Paul's story about the ease with which the fire started, the unusually rapid pace at which it spread, and that he would have exited the house without first ensuring his parents' safety. Paul was charged with two counts of first-degree murder, as well as arson and insurance fraud. In an interview for an episode of the television series *Forensic Files* (Duffield, 2005), he said: "I was horrified. It felt like I was in my own horror film."

Paul hired defense attorneys who, in turn, hired experts to counter the conclusions of the fire investigation and offer reasonable explanations for the so-called evidence. Through chemical testing, elaborate re-creations, and other scientific analysis, these experts managed to convince the court that the prior conclusions were totally wrong and, in fact, everything that Paul said had happened made perfect sense. It turned out that the fire reacted with the polyurethane fabric on the sofa exactly as would be expected, and the gasoline evidence on the floor was the result of a practice in the 1970s— when the house was built—by flooring contractors who would stretch their supply of varnish by cutting it with leaded gasoline. This explained why no gasoline was found *on top of* the carpet, which presumably would be the case if it had been poured for use as an accelerant. Plus, the fact that it was *leaded* gasoline (which had already been mostly phased out in the United States by then) corroborated the improbability of any malicious intent. After spending ten months in jail and facing a possible death sentence, all charges were dropped against Paul and he walked out a free man.

Paul Camiolo was somewhat more fortunate than Patricia "Patti" Stallings, who was wrongfully convicted of murdering her four-month-old son. In 1989, Patti and her husband, David, of St. Louis, Missouri, worried about baby Ryan, who seemed to be constantly sick since birth with no clear cause. When he seemed to take a turn for the worse one day in September, Patti decided to take him to the emergency room. Once there, the stumped doctors took blood samples and sent them to an outside lab for testing. When the results came back indicating high levels of ethylene glycol (the active ingredient in antifreeze), hospital staff called the authorities and started Ryan on an ethanol drip in an attempt to combat the effects of the poison. Ryan soon recovered enough to be released into foster care, but it wasn't long before he got sick again, which happened to be soon after a supervised visit with Patti. He again was rushed to the hospital, where ethylene glycol was found at even higher levels than the last time. That finding led to Patti's arrest and incarceration as she awaited trial on an assault charge, which was upgraded to murder when baby Ryan died a week later.

About five months after Ryan's death, while Patti was still awaiting trial, she gave birth to another baby, whom the couple named David Jr. (calling him "DJ" for short). DJ was immediately placed in foster care, and when he got sick a few weeks later, he was rushed to a different hospital. There, he was diagnosed with methylmalonic acidemia (MMA), a rare genetic condition that produces a toxin in the blood called propionic acid (a compound that differs from ethylene glycol by only one atom). Despite DJ's diagnosis, Patti was found guilty of first-degree murder in Ryan's death and sentenced to life in prison without the possibility of parole. The case eventually gained the attention of scientists who offered to retest the samples. Sure enough, when the samples were retested with MMA in mind, it was clear that baby Ryan died of the same condition that afflicted DJ. In fact, the treatment Ryan received in the hospital that was based on his misdiagnosis very likely contributed to his death (Fields and Johnston, 2010, p. 32). After being incarcerated for nearly two years, Patti was exonerated and set free in 1991. The family subsequently settled several lawsuits out of court, and DJ apparently managed life with the disease until his death in 2013 at the age of 23.

The Camiolo and Stallings cases serve as reminders that every incident involving a human death should be examined and investigated with fresh eyes and only by qualified experts. Just because an incident may resemble one (or many) seen before does not mean that they can be treated as the same. Making assumptions, cutting corners, and failing to ask questions are some fundamental reasons that many covertly committed murders are overlooked and that innocent people are occasionally convicted of murders they did not commit—or that never happened in the first place.

In the *Forensic Files* episode on the Camiolo case (Duffield, 2005), defense attorney Thomas S. Cometa offered an explanation that also lends insight into what can happen in other cases like this: "I'm not saying that it was malicious and intentional," he said. "I'm saying that, unfortunately, [the investigators] had gut feelings and years of practical experience that led them to conclude this *had to be* an arson fire. So, they let common perceptions outweigh logic and science, and, luckily, logic and science prevailed in this case." No one should have to rely on *luck* when standing trial for their life.

These cases also illustrate the fact that mistakes are likely to occur when people are put in charge of investigations that require skills and knowledge they do not possess. Members of the public (and, thus, juries) may falsely believe that medical doctors are infallible and that fields like fire investigation are an exact science, prompting them to automatically accept the conclusions of these so-called "experts." However, all sciences are *inexact*, in that none is infallible and all require continuous evaluation and refinement to make progress.

In fact, many people may not realize that most fire investigators are essentially midcareer firefighters, not scientists, and that this distinction is an important one. John Lentini, a nationally recognized fire expert who helped with the Camiolo defense, said of fire investigation: "It's a matter of a profession that is largely controlled and dominated by hacks. And these people didn't set out to become hacks, but they don't know what they're doing. They're making complicated decisions about chemistry and physics, and they never took chemistry and physics" (Duffield, 2005).

Other inexact sciences include forensic dentistry, which has been implicated in multiple overturned murder convictions that were based on bitemark evidence, as well as psychiatry and much of the trace-evidence analysis done in crime labs such as comparisons of synthetic fibers and hair samples without attached roots (where the genetic material is found). In many of these cases, experts can only truly say whether the evidence is *consistent with* or *inconsistent with* the standard or example to which it is being compared.

Lastly, many people may not be aware that a medical examiner is not the same as a coroner. While a medical examiner is a physician with board certification in a medical specialty (often pathology), a coroner is typically an elected layperson who may or may not have any particular education, training, or certification. Depending on the jurisdiction, either one can make official pronouncements that appear on death certificates, steer investigations, and sway juries. Perhaps establishing clearer standards and more sensible criteria to qualify someone as an expert would be a good place to start making important changes.

## References

Amnesty International. (2022). *Amnesty International global report: Death sentences and executions 2021.* https://www.amnesty.org/en/documents/act50/5418/2022/en/

Bauer, L., Broady, K.E., Edelberg, W., and O'Donnell, J. (2020, September 17). *Ten facts about COVID-19 and the U.S. economy.* Brookings Institution. https://www.brookings.edu/wp-content/uploads/2020/09/FutureShutdowns_Facts_LO_Final.pdf

Brenan, M. (2020, August 12). Amid pandemic, confidence in key U.S. institutions surges. *Gallup.* https://news.gallup.com/poll/317135/amid-pandemic-confidence-key-institutions-surges.aspx

Czeisler, M.E., Lane, R.I., Petrosky, E., Wiley, J.F., Christensen, A., Njai, R., et al. (2020, August 14). Mental health, substance use, and suicidal ideation during the COVID-19 pandemic—United States, June 24–30, 2020. *Morbidity and Mortality Weekly Report, 69*(32), 1049–1057. https://www.cdc.gov/mmwr/volumes/69/wr/mm6932a1.htm

Dimock, M., and Wike, R. (2020, November 13). America is exceptional in the nature of its political divide. *Pew Research Center.* https://www.pewresearch.org/fact-tank/2020/11/13/america-is-exceptional-in-the-nature-of-its-political-divide/

Duffield, M. (Senior Editor). (2005, June 29). Up in smoke (Season 10, Episode 4) [TV series episode]. In P. Dowling (Executive Producer), *Forensic Files.* Medstar Television.

Fields, S., and Johnston, M. (2010). *Genetic twists of fate.* Cambridge, MA: MIT Press.

Fox, J.A., and Levin, J. (1994). Firing back: The growing threat of workplace homicide. *ANNALS of the American Academy of Political and Social Science, 536*(1), 16–30.

Geiger, A.W. (2018, July 4). How Americans see their country and their democracy. *Pew Research Center.* https://www.pewresearch.org/fact-tank/2018/07/04/how-americans-see-their-country-and-their-democracy/

Horowitz, J.M., Igielnik, R., and Kochhar, R. (2020, January 9). Trends in income and wealth inequality. *Pew Research Center.* https://www.pewsocialtrends.org/2020/01/09/trends-in-income-and-wealth-inequality/#fnref-27657-13

Khurshid, A., Ahmad, H., Jaffry, A.A., Khurshid, M., and Ali, G. (2022). A homicide in disguise: How the autopsy dug up clues. *Cureus, 14*(5). https://doi.org/10.7759/cureus.24691

Levine, S. (2000, December 31). Mask of old age hides killings. *Washington Post.* https://www.washingtonpost.com/archive/politics/2000/12/31/mask-of-old-age-hides-killings/c4d7d0f8-95a0-408c-89b3-37e4a10e0318/

Madfis, E. (2020). *How to stop school rampage killing: Lessons from averted mass shootings and bombings* (2nd ed.). Palgrave Macmillan.

McPherson, M., Smith-Lovin, L., and Brashears, M.E. (2006). Social isolation in America: Changes in core discussion networks over two decades. *American Sociological Review, 71*(3), 353–375.

National Registry of Exonerations. (2021, June 14). *25,000 years lost to wrongful convictions.* https://www.law.umich.edu/special/exoneration/Documents/25000%20Years.pdf

Panchal, N., Kamal, R., Orgera, K., Cox, C., Garfield, R., Hamel, L., et al. (2020, August 21). The implications of COVID-19 for mental health and substance use. *Kaiser Family Foundation.* https://www.kff.org/coronavi rus-covid-19/issue-brief/the-implications-of-covid-19-for-mental-hea lth-and-substance-use/

Parker, K., Morin, R., and Horowitz, J.M. (2019, March 21). Looking to the future, public sees an America in decline on many fronts. *Pew Research Center.* https://www.pewsocialtrends.org/2019/03/21/public-sees-an-america-in-decline-on-many-fronts/

Robb, C.E., de Jager, C.A., Ahmadi-Abhari, S., Giannakopoulou, P., Udeh-Momoh, C., McKeand, J., et al. (2020, September 17). Associations of social isolation with anxiety and depression during the early COVID-19 pandemic: A survey of older adults in London, UK. *Frontiers in Psychiatry, 11.* https://www.frontiersin.org/articles/10.3389/fpsyt.2020.591120/full

Schaeffer, K. (2020, February 7). 6 facts about economic inequality in the U.S. *Pew Research Center.* https://www.pewresearch.org/fact-tank/2020/02/07/6-facts-about-economic-inequality-in-the-u-s/

Vogels, E.A. (2021, January 13). The state of online harassment. *Pew Research Center.* https://www.pewresearch.org/internet/2021/01/13/the-state-of-online-harassment/

APPENDIX

# Case Summaries

Using the Nexis database of newspapers and newswires across the United States, we collected the following 37 cases covering a three-year period (June 2017 to July 2020) in which a death that was originally classified as something other than homicide was subsequently reclassified as homicide.

## David Schlachet (Vincent and Dorn, 2020)

In July 2018, the superintendent at 48-year-old Lara Prychodko's Manhattan apartment building found her mangled body in the trash compactor after an apparent 27-flight fall down the garbage chute. Authorities said she had an abnormally high alcohol level in her system and ruled it a "fatal accident." A year later, however, New York City former chief medical examiner Michael Baden agreed to take another look. Finding indications that Prychodko had been strangled to death before being placed into the chute, as well as seeing little bleeding from lacerations sustained in the fall, the doctor concluded that the manner of death was most likely homicide. Moreover, Baden said the fact that Prychodko's body was found topless would be unusual in an accident scenario and might be evidence that a struggle took place. At the time of her death, Lara and her estranged husband were in the midst of a highly contentious divorce, even though 55-year-old David Schlachet's construction company continued to struggle after a 2016 bankruptcy. He had also been ordered to pay alimony and attorney fees to Prychodko, who was favored to gain child custody and a percentage of their millions of dollars in assets.

## Karl Karlsen (Flynn, 2020)

Karl Karlsen's first wife, 30-year-old Christina, died in a January 1991 house fire in Murphys, California. When the fire broke out, she was trapped in a bathroom behind a boarded-up window and had no way to escape the conflagration. Firefighters ruled the blaze accidental, and Karl Karlsen collected $200,000 in life insurance that he had taken out on Christina

131

shortly before her death. He then moved with his children across the country to Varick, New York and remarried. In November 2008, he killed his son by making a truck slip off its jack while the 23-year-old was underneath it, crushing him to death. This, too, was officially ruled a tragic accident. However, when his second wife learned of the hefty life insurance policy her husband had taken out on his son's life, she became suspicious and hired an investigator, who found that Karl had an even larger insurance policy on her life. With this information, she went to the police and ended up wearing a wire to record Karl admitting that he killed his son. Karl was charged with murder in the second degree, to which he pleaded guilty on the same day his trial was scheduled to begin in 2013. This case led the California authorities to take another look at the death of his first wife, and the reinvestigation resulted in his conviction for first-degree murder in February 2020, nearly 30 years after the fatal fire.

## Chad Daybell (Donaldson, 2020)

When 49-year-old Tammy Daybell died in her sleep at her Salem, Idaho, home in October 2019, it initially looked like natural causes. No autopsy was ordered and nothing seemed suspicious—until her husband Chad remarried just two weeks later. That's when police reopened their investigation and quickly uncovered several red flags. Not only had Chad taken out a large insurance policy on Tammy's life, but his new wife, Lori Vallow, had become a widow a few months earlier and now appeared not to know the location of her two children, seven-year-old J.J. Vallow and 16-year-old Tylee Ryan. In July 2019, Lori's brother shot her husband to death in alleged self-defense, but just as investigators began to take another look, the brother died in December 2019 of what was later determined to be natural causes. In May 2021, both Chad and Lori were indicted on first-degree murder and other charges in relation to the deaths of her children, and each was also charged with killing their respective former spouse. Lori was tried first and found guilty in May 2023, at which time Chad's trial was still unscheduled.

## Nathanial Ridnour (*The Telegraph Herald*, 2020)

In 2004, 17-year-old Nathanial Ridnour was not the boy that his 15-year-old girlfriend's grandmother thought was good for her granddaughter, and Bonnie Callahan, 73, wasn't shy about voicing her objections to the relationship. Shortly after Ridnour argued with Callahan in her Manchester, Iowa, apartment in June of that year, someone apparently beat Callahan to death and then put her body into the Mississippi River. When she was found the next day, the authorities thought it looked like an accidental drowning and did not initially suspect foul play, despite the autopsy report noting signs of blunt-force trauma. The case went cold for more than a decade, until Iowa's Major Crime Unit and the local police reopened the investigation in 2017. In May 2020, they charged 34-year-old Ridnour with first-degree murder in relation to Callahan's death. However, a jury subsequently declared Ridnour not guilty and he was set free in December 2021.

## Reta Mays (Kennedy and Schwartz, 2020)

At least seven patients in a medical center for veterans in West Virginia died in mysterious circumstances between July 2017 and June 2018. Even though Reta Mays seemed to be nearby each time, the deaths were initially assumed to be due to natural causes. However, once the number grew too large to explain away, suspicion fell on the 46-year-old nursing assistant. It was eventually discovered that when Mays worked in a ward that housed many patients who had diabetes, she would sometimes inject a lethal dose of insulin into others who were not diabetic, causing their blood sugar levels to plummet. Mays admitted to her crimes in 2020, pleading guilty to seven counts of second-degree murder and one count of attempted murder. In May 2021, she received seven life sentences—one for each murder—plus an additional 20 years for the eighth victim whose life she had tried to take.

## Frank Buschauer (Vitello, 2019)

Frank Buschauer drowned his 47-year-old wife of three years in the bathtub of their South Barrington, Illinois, home in February 2000. He pulled her body out sometime later and laid her on the bedroom floor. He then called 911, saying that he had woken up in the middle of the night and found her underwater and unconscious in the tub, and pulled her out. The case was initially ruled a drowning of undetermined origin, but the medical examiner failed to find an epileptic attack, seizure, heat stroke, or any other undiagnosed pathology. Twelve years later, prosecutors reopened the cold case and asked another medical examiner to review the autopsy findings. That doctor changed the manner of death to homicide, later testifying that there were bruises on the victim's nose and chin, and abrasions on the knuckles of her hands, suggesting that there had been an altercation around the time of her death. Prosecutors brought first-degree murder charges against Buschauer in 2013 and he was eventually convicted in 2019. He was sentenced the following year to 25 years in prison.

## Jason T. Harris (Thompson, 2019)

Thirty-nine-year-old Jason T. Harris, from Davison, Michigan, may have wanted to kill his 36-year-old wife, Christina, to avoid getting divorced and having to pay child support. In addition, if she happened to die by natural or accidental causes, he would receive $120,000 in life insurance proceeds. After allegedly trying to hire someone to kill Christina without success, Jason was accused of putting a fatal dose of heroin in her cereal one morning in September 2014. Because Christina was not a known drug user, friends and family were suspicious and urged police to investigate further. Five years after Christina's death was ruled an accidental overdose, the medical examiner changed the manner of death to homicide, and Jason was arrested. In November 2021, he was convicted of murdering his wife and was sentenced the following month to life in prison without the possibility of parole.

## Ray Neal (Harris, 2019)

In July 2019, 61-year-old Ray Neal was found dead in a bedroom of his Lawrenceville, Georgia, home after his sister told the authorities that she hadn't heard from him in days. Despite investigators finding blood spatter in multiple locations throughout the home, the Gwinnett County Medical Examiner's Office concluded that it was a natural death—a decision likely swayed by the fact that Neal had multiple chronic health conditions and an alleged history of drug use. Several days later, funeral home employees noticed stab wounds in Neal's neck that had apparently been overlooked during the original examination. The manner of death was changed to undetermined while investigators re-examined the case, and the medical examiner's office officially ruled it a homicide in October 2020. No suspect had been identified at the time of writing.

## Ali Elmezayen (Fieldstadt, 2019)

Ali Elmezayen, 44, of South Bay, California, was convicted of more than a dozen federal charges and sent to prison for more than 200 years—all before standing trial on murder and attempted murder charges that stemmed from the same incident. In April 2015, Elmezayen is alleged to have intentionally driven his car off a pier at the Port of Los Angeles with his ex-wife and two of their three sons inside. His wife managed to escape to safety, but the boys, ages 13 and eight, both of whom had autism, drowned. Four years after the incident was ruled an accident, the federal authorities arrested Elmezayen after discovering that he had purchased accidental death insurance worth more than $3 million on his family members. He was found guilty in October 2019 of aggravated identity theft (for impersonating his ex-wife in dealings with the insurance companies), as well as multiple counts of mail fraud, wire fraud, and money laundering. In March 2021, he was sentenced to 212 years in federal prison and ordered to pay $261,751 in restitution to the defrauded insurers. Although the Los Angeles County district attorney's office initially declined to prosecute the case, the federal indictment apparently prompted second thoughts, as Elmezayen was charged in July 2019 with two counts of capital murder and one count of attempted murder. No trial date had been set at the time of writing.

## Patrick Melbourne (Divine, 2019)

There was never enough evidence to charge Patrick Melbourne with killing Jerrilynn Mullins, of Oakdale, Minnesota—or even to find him civilly liable—but the jury in a 1989 wrongful death suit against him did conclude that Mullins had been murdered. The 28-year-old newlywed was last seen on the evening of November 15, 1978, riding off with Melbourne in his car. Mullins had been invited by her husband to meet him and some business associates for a drink after work, and a smaller group eventually decided to go elsewhere for dinner. They took just two cars to the restaurant about 20 miles away, and Melbourne supposedly was giving Mullins a ride back to her car at the end of the evening. Her decomposed body was found in a swampy area just over seven months later, but no cause of death could be determined after two autopsies. The manner of death was listed as undetermined for 11 years until the civil case established it as homicide. Melbourne, who had an extensive criminal history spanning both before and after the death of Mullins, died in 2015; the cold case is still considered open.

## Linda Roberts and Mary Tomaselli (Swenson, 2019)

In March 2015, a pair of sisters in Palm Harbor, Florida, killed their 85-year-old father, Anthony Tomaselli. When Mary Tomaselli, then 59, and Linda Roberts, then 57, called for paramedics, they at first claimed to have found their father unresponsive as they tried to resuscitate him. The man's numerous health problems—including a history of cancer, dementia, and heart problems—likely supported the initial determination of death by natural causes, especially in the absence of an autopsy. Four years later, however, a man who was romantically linked to both sisters provided the authorities with a recording of the women confessing to planning and carrying out their father's murder by suffocation (after first attempting to poison him). Both were charged with first-degree murder in March 2019 and each pleaded guilty two years later to second-degree murder. Tomaselli was sentenced to 15 years in prison and Roberts received 20 years.

## Elaine Hurd (O'Cain, 2019)

In June 2017, Elaine Hurd brought her two-year-old son to her boyfriend's Spokane, Washington, home, where the boy suffered a serious head injury after the couple claimed he accidentally fell down the stairs. Hurd then put the toddler to bed for the night, but did not seek medical care until she found him the next morning having a seizure. The boy was hospitalized in a coma for weeks until he died, although a neurosurgeon who had treated the child said he would have survived had he received prompt medical attention. What at first appeared to be a tragic accident ended up being classified as homicide after a medical examiner's report questioned whether the child's head injury could have been sustained in a fall. About a year after the incident, in July 2018, Hurd was arrested and charged with killing her son. She ultimately accepted a plea deal and was convicted of second-degree criminal mistreatment. In June 2019, she was sentenced to 12 months in jail.

## Theresa Bentaas (Leader, 2019)

In February 1981, the body of a newborn baby was found in a ditch in Sioux Falls, South Dakota. The cause of death was determined to be exposure, but whether the circumstances were intentional or accidental was unclear. In February 2019, almost exactly 38 years after the grim discovery, the authorities, using genetic genealogy, linked the baby's DNA to a 57-year-old woman named Theresa Bentaas, who still lived in the area and worked as a paralegal. Bentaas eventually confessed that she became pregnant at the age of 19, kept it a secret until she gave birth alone in her apartment, and then abandoned the hours-old infant in the ditch. She was arrested in March 2019 and charged with murder. In December 2021, she was sentenced to ten years in prison, but with nine years suspended and credit for time served.

## Joshua Hunsucker (Llamas, 2019)

In September 2018, 32-year-old Stacy Hunsucker died in her Mount Holly, North Carolina, home from what looked like a heart attack. The married mother of two had a history of heart problems, so the cause of death was not initially questioned. However, the subsequent behavior of Joshua Hunsucker, a 34-year-old paramedic at the time of his wife's death, raised suspicions that eventually led to an investigation. Not only did he refuse an autopsy and insist on having her body cremated, but he also tried to immediately collect on a hefty life insurance policy and seemed to have moved on with a new girlfriend rather quickly. However, because Stacy was an organ donor, a blood sample had been collected and stored before the cremation. Toxicology testing revealed a high level of tetrahydrozoline, a chemical commonly found in eyedrops and nasal sprays that can be lethal if ingested. Joshua was arrested in December 2019 and charged with murdering his wife. He appeared in court for pretrial motions in January 2022, when the judge also issued a gag order forbidding anyone directly involved in the case from publicly discussing it.

## Adam Shacknai (Repard, 2019)

In July 2011, six-year-old Max Shacknai suffered fatal injuries after an accidental fall over a second-floor banister inside a beach house mansion near San Diego, California. At the time, Max was under the care of Rebecca Zahau, the 32-year-old girlfriend of the boy's father, Jonah Shacknai, who was then the CEO of Medicis Pharmaceutical. Two days after the tragic accident, while Shacknai kept vigil by his son's hospital bed, his brother, Adam, called the authorities to report finding Zahau's body hanging from a balcony at the mansion; she was nude, gagged, and bound at the wrists and ankles. Although Zahau's death was officially ruled a suicide, her family believed that Adam Shacknai was responsible and filed a wrongful death civil lawsuit against him. In April 2018, a jury agreed with the family and awarded them $5 million in damages (which was later reduced to $600,000 on appeal).

## Rexford Lynn Keel (Bonvillian, 2019)

In March 2019, the body of 38-year-old Diana Keel was found with stab wounds in a wooded area near her Nashville, North Carolina, home just days after being reported missing. When authorities arrested her husband, 57-year-old Rexford Lynn Keel, and learned that his first wife had died in what looked like a freak accident, they became suspicious enough to reopen the earlier case as a possible homicide. Elizabeth Keel, 42, died on New Year's Day 2006 from blunt-force trauma to the head. At the time, her surviving spouse said that the fatal injury was caused by Elizabeth hitting forehead in a fall down the concrete front steps of their home. In October 2021, Rexford Lynn Keel received a prison sentence of 32 to 41 years after pleading guilty to second-degree murder and first-degree kidnapping in his second wife's death; the investigation into his first wife's death is still ongoing.

## Unnamed physician (Weiner, 2019)

When 72-year-old Penelope Holloway was found dead in September 2018 inside her Arlington, Virginia, home, the cause was initially thought to be natural. However, at the urging of a friend, the authorities pursued an investigation and eventually determined that Holloway died after being drugged and then smothered. Many suspected that her death was the result of physician-assisted suicide, and it was officially ruled a homicide the following April. Because the unnamed physician who apparently played a role in Holloway's death had died a few days afterward, no one was prosecuted.

## Roderick Covlin (Ransom, 2019)

In December 2009, Roderick Covlin, then 36, sneaked into his 47-year-old estranged wife's New York City apartment and strangled her to death. He then placed Shele Danishefsky's body in her bathtub, filled it with water, and attempted to stage the scene to look like a tragic slip-and-fall. The couple's nine-year-old daughter found her mother's body the following morning. Danishefsky's death was treated as an accidental drowning, and no autopsy was performed until her body was exhumed months later at the urging of her family. The manner of death was changed to homicide at that point, but it was another six years until Covlin was arrested in November 2015. In establishing Covlin's motive at trial, prosecutors said that Danishefsky—who was far wealthier than her soon-to-be-ex—planned to cut him out of her will the day after she was killed. Covlin was convicted of second-degree murder in March 2019 and subsequently received the maximum sentence of 25 years to life in prison.

## Thomas Foster (Gambardello, 2019)

Because of her advanced age and complex medical history, 85-year-old Carolyn Foster's death in January 2019 was initially ruled to be due to natural causes. But then a relative came forward and told police that Carolyn's 63-year-old son, Thomas—who shared her Manchester Township, New Jersey, home—had intentionally killed her. Based on this, as well as the results of an autopsy that indicated trauma to her neck and ribs, county prosecutors and local police reopened the investigation. Thomas was arrested in July and charged with murdering his mother. Although prosecutors said he admitted to pressing "very hard" on his mother's neck and punching her in the throat, the defense countered that he was only trying to revive her. As of September 2019, Thomas was on home supervision while awaiting trial, but no scheduled start date could be found.

## Peter Romans (*Noticias Financieras*, 2019)

Peter Romans, then 48, was the sole survivor in the April 2008 house fire in Madison County, Ohio, that claimed the lives of his wife and their two children, ages 12 and 16, in what looked like a terrible accident. The fire had spread to the rental home after starting in the family's Ford Expedition, which had a potentially faulty switch that was part of a recall at the time but had not been repaired. However, when the blaze was ruled to be arson in August 2009, the three deaths officially became homicides. Still, it wasn't until July 2019—more than 11 years after the fatal fire—that Romans was arrested and charged with multiple counts of murder and aggravated arson. In lieu of a jury trial, Romans opted for a three-judge panel to decide his fate, and he was found not guilty in October 2020.

## Samuel Little (Hickman, 2019)

When 34-year-old Martha Cunningham's bruised and partially nude body was discovered in a wooded area near Knoxville, Tennessee, in January 1975, investigators initially regarded her cause of death as natural. There were no stab marks or bullet wounds, and the bruises could be explained away by her history of seizures. However, in October 2019—nearly half a century after Cunningham was killed—her death officially became a homicide when recently captured serial killer Samuel Little confessed to driving her to the outskirts of town and strangling her in his car. Little was never charged with Cunningham's murder, mainly because he was already serving life in prison without the possibility of parole in California after being convicted in 2014 of three other murders. In December 2020, Little died at the age of 80.

## Randolph Garbutt (Logan, 2019)

Randolph Garbutt, then 38, and Raven Campbell, 31, were roommates in a publicly subsidized apartment in Lomita, California, when Campbell suddenly went missing in June 2009. She remained missing for six years, with Garbutt claiming ignorance of her whereabouts, until a tip-off from a mutual friend led to the discovery of her body hidden inside a closet wall. Garbutt had bludgeoned his roommate in the head with a hammer before wrapping her body in plastic, placing her in a hole in the wall, and then covering the hole with a large poster. Campbell's body was found in July 2015 and Garbutt was arrested about seven months later. In court, he pleaded no contest to manslaughter and was sentenced in October 2019 to 11 years in prison.

## Nancy Moronez (Moreno, 2018)

Nancy Moronez apparently could not tolerate crying babies. At least, that was the reason she gave for killing her two-week-old infant when unexpectedly confessing to her grown daughter 35 years after the fact. This 1980 murder in Franklin, Wisconsin, was the first of three committed by Moronez, who later claimed that each infant had been crying nonstop before she decided to silence them forever. She drowned her first victim in the bathtub, and the next two—both infants whom she was babysitting—were suffocated, one in 1984 and one the year after. Each death was ruled a case of sudden infant death syndrome (SIDS), and it wasn't until her spontaneous confession in March 2015 that there was finally evidence of murder. Moronez ended up confessing to the two additional murders and was finally charged for all three in February 2018. A year later, a judge sentenced the 62-year-old to three consecutive ten-year prison terms.

## Anna Elizabeth Young (Brasch, 2018)

Anna Elizabeth Young was in her 40s when she became the leader of a religious cult near Gainesville, Florida, called the House of Prayer for All People, which operated from 1983 until 1992. During that time, many members were abused, and several children went missing. Although Young served a six-month sentence in the 1990s for child abuse—she used bleach to bathe a 12-year-old member—she wasn't charged with homicides committed in the late 1980s until decades later. After Young's adult daughter came forward to police, following which Young was arrested in November 2017 and charged in the deaths of two children, one who had been presumed missing (his body was never found) and the other thought to have died from natural causes. She was eventually convicted of second-degree murder in the death of a toddler who had been locked in a closet and starved, as well as manslaughter for withholding medication from a two-year-old who suffered a fatal seizure. She died in prison in early 2021, just about six weeks after receiving a 30-year sentence.

## Lewis Bennett (Flynn, 2018)

In May 2017, Lewis Bennett, then 40, took his 41-year-old wife of just three months, Isabella Hellmann, of Delray Beach, Florida, on a sailing trip for a belated honeymoon. A few days into the trip and just west of the Bahamas, Bennett said he awoke during the night to a loud crash and his wife nowhere to be found. With the 40-foot catamaran taking on water, Bennett escaped on a life raft and was rescued a few hours later. A four-day search failed to find Hellmann, making what was assumed to be a terrible accident even worse. Bennett later became a suspect when he attempted to have Hellmann declared legally dead so that he could gain access to her property and other assets. In February 2018, he was charged with second-degree murder, but later agreed to a plea deal that included a conviction for involuntary manslaughter and an eight-year prison sentence. Hellmann's body was never found, but she was officially declared dead in May 2019.

## Nickalas Kedrowitz (Bever, 2018)

In a span of less than three months in 2017, 13-year-old Nickalas Kedrowitz's family had to bury his two-year-old sister and one-year-old stepbrother—in May and July, respectively—each of whom was found lifeless after being babysat in their Osgood, Indiana, home by their teenage sibling. Nickalas called 911 in both cases, but was too late. Also in both cases, an autopsy was performed, but offered inconclusive results. Two months after the second death, the teenager's mother called police after discovering that he had mutilated two kittens; upon questioning, Nickalas admitted suffocating his siblings. He was found guilty in August 2021 on two counts of murder and was subsequently sentenced to 100 years in prison.

## Philip Snider (*Associated Press*, 2018)

In January 2018, 73-year-old Philip Snider struck his wife of 53 years, Roberta, 70, in the head with a two-pound stake hammer as she slept on the loveseat in their Hartville, Ohio, home. After disposing of her body, he concocted a bizarre story to tell anyone who inquired about her welfare or whereabouts that involved a fictitious road trip to Graceland in Memphis, Tennessee, during which Roberta died of natural causes and was cremated. Seven months later, Philip pleaded guilty to aggravated murder in a deal that required him to disclose where he had disposed of his wife's body in exchange for a prison sentence of 20 years to life.

## Stephany Elizabeth LaFountain (Bonvillian, 2018)

Stephany Elizabeth LaFountain, of Fairbanks, Alaska, was 20 years old when her four-month-old daughter died in September 2015. The cause was officially undetermined, but was thought to be an accident—that is, until her 13-month-old daughter died a little more than two years later. The November 2017 death was investigated more thoroughly than the first, and the authorities concluded that the infant had been deliberately suffocated. This finding led to the reopening of the previous case and LaFountain's subsequent arrest in August 2018, when she was charged with first- and second-degree murder in each infant's death. Her trial was set to begin in September 2019, but has been delayed multiple times; at the time of writing, it is scheduled for September 2023.

## Debbie Siers-Hill (Weiner, 2018)

When Debbie Siers-Hill, 63, of Virginia Beach, Virginia, was given a nearly three-year prison sentence in January 2019 for possessing ricin, that was apparently the best prosecutors could manage after the mysterious death of Siers-Hill's boyfriend in February 2016. Both the cause and manner of 67-year-old Frederick M. Brooks' death were officially undetermined, but his family members soon suspected Siers-Hill—especially after learning that her husband had died in 1993 of an apparent suicide after drinking antifreeze. About a month after Brooks died, a search of Siers-Hill's storage unit uncovered the ricin and several other suspicious items, including a syringe laced with the deadly poison, a packet of castor plant seeds, and latex gloves. The authorities said that she also possessed a quantity of powdered caffeine and had researched caffeine poisoning on the internet.

## Denise Williams (Fineout, 2018)

Denise Williams, of Tallahassee, Florida, was 30 years old in December 2000 when her 31-year-old husband, Mike Williams, was killed in an apparent hunting accident. Denise was also having an affair with her husband's best friend, Brian Winchester, who was duck hunting with Mike when he apparently fell out of their boat and was eaten by alligators. His body was never found. However, 16 years after Mike's death, Winchester came forward and told police the truth: that he took his friend on the hunting trip, shot him in the face, and buried his body. He said that he and Denise had planned the killing so they could collect a hefty insurance payout, and he offered to testify against her in exchange for immunity from prosecution. In December 2018, a jury found Denise, now 48, guilty of murder and conspiracy, and she was sentenced to life in prison plus 30 years. Although the murder conviction and life sentence were later overturned on appeal, the conspiracy conviction was upheld. For that, a judge resentenced Denise in September 2021 to 30 years in prison.

## Stanley C. Burkhardt (Becker, 2018)

In August 1982, a 17-year-old boy who was known to hustle men on the streets of New Orleans was found dead in the Mississippi River. An autopsy revealed the cause of death to be drowning with an undetermined manner, but Detective Stanley C. Burkhardt—who is credited with starting the New Orleans Police Department's Pedophile Unit—insisted that it had been a homicide. That same detective was fired and imprisoned in 1987 after sending pornographic images of underage boys to undercover federal agents, the first of multiple prison terms he served in subsequent decades for child pornography and molestation convictions. By 2011, the federal authorities determined that Burkhardt met the conditions to be legally deemed "sexually dangerous," which would subject him to lifetime federal supervision and indefinite confinement. However, after four years of incarceration, he was conditionally released in 2015 and managed to stay out of trouble for the next few years. In 2018—36 years after the teenager's death—Burkhardt became a suspect when two men separately came forward claiming that the former detective had abused them in the 1970s. Each also said that Burkhardt would threaten him to stay quiet while bragging about boys he had killed—including the teenager found in the river—and even showing crime scene photos to prove it. Investigators subsequently reopened the 1982 case, as well as three others from the late 1970s in which teenage boys were killed in similar circumstances. In July 2019, the now-68-year-old Burkhardt was arrested again for violating the terms of sex offender registry laws, and a judge subsequently found that he had violated the terms of his conditional release and reinstated the indefinite confinement. At the time of writing, he remains in custody and has not been charged in relation to any death.

## Tieray Jones (Wheeler, 2018)

In April 2002, Tieray Jones, 26, claimed that his two-year-old stepson disappeared from a park in San Diego, California. He was the toddler's primary caregiver while his wife—the child's mother—was at sea with the Navy. The boy's body was never found and no witnesses could be found to verify Jones' story, though residents of the apartment complex where Jones lived said they observed him carrying three large trash bags to a dumpster around the same time that the toddler disappeared. In April 2016, Jones was finally arrested and charged with murder. After his trial ended in a deadlocked jury, a judge dismissed the charge against him in March 2018.

## Lana Clayton (Swenson, 2018)

In July 2018, 64-year-old Steven Clayton's body was found sprawled on the foyer floor of his Lake Wylie, South Carolina, home. The authorities initially believed that he had tumbled down the stairs after a possible heart attack, but his family became suspicious of his wife's apparently strange behavior in the aftermath and requested an autopsy and toxicology test. Results of the blood screening revealed a toxic level of tetrahydrozoline, the active ingredient in over-the-counter eyedrops. When confronted with the evidence, Lana Clayton, 52, confessed that she had placed eyedrops in her husband's water over several days, but insisted that she only intended to harm him and not to cause his death. Lana pleaded guilty to voluntary manslaughter in January 2020 and was sentenced to 25 years in prison.

# Ronald Bailey (Jany, 2018)

The authorities in Minneapolis, Minnesota, initially thought 61-year-old Riley Housley's January 2018 death was the result of an accidental fall. His girlfriend reported finding him in his home seated upright, but bleeding and barely conscious. When she asked him if he knew what happened, Housley muttered one word: "Ron." Police later found a bloody hammer in the laundry room, as well as surveillance video that showed Housley's friend Ronald Bailey, 53, entering and re-entering the home several times that day. After an autopsy concluded that Housley died from blunt-force head trauma, his death was ruled a homicide. Bailey was charged with second-degree murder in February 2018.

# Angelika Graswald (Rojas, 2017)

In April 2015, 35-year-old Angelika Graswald and her fiancé, Vincent Viafore, went on a kayaking excursion down the Hudson River—a trip that only Graswald survived. The authorities at first sided with Graswald in her claim that Viafore drowned after his kayak capsized in rough waters and she was unable to save him. But finding the drain plug to Viafore's kayak in Graswald's car and discovering that she was the beneficiary of his two life insurance policies later led them to believe that she had sabotaged the kayak in a deliberate plot to cause his death. Graswald was charged with second-degree murder in 2015, but ended up pleading guilty in July 2017 to criminally negligent homicide. In November 2017, she was sentenced to 16 months to four years in prison and was given credit for time served; she was released on parole about six weeks later.

# John Bittrolff (Eltman, 2017)

John Bittrolff, a 51-year-old Long Island, New York, carpenter, was convicted in July 2017 of killing two sex workers in 1993 and 1994. The nude bodies of Rita Tangredi, 31, and Colleen McNamee, 20, were found nine miles apart in a wooded area near Bittrolff's property. Although at first they were assumed to be victims of an active serial killer in the area, Bittrolff later became a suspect when investigators linked his DNA to the two women's bodies. Bittrolff was sentenced to two consecutive prison terms of 25 years to life.

# Joaquin Rams (Barakat, 2017)

In October 2012, 40-year-old Joaquin Rams, of Manassas, Virginia, held his 15-month-old son's head under running water until he drowned. He then called 911 and reported finding the child inexplicably unresponsive. Although the boy had apparently suffered several seizures in the months leading up to his death, the fatal incident occurred during a court-ordered unsupervised visit to which the boy's mother had objected. In April 2017, Rams was convicted of murder and sentenced to life in prison without parole. His apparent motive was to collect on a more than $500,000 insurance policy on his son's life.

## References

*Associated Press.* (2018, August 27). Man pleads guilty to murder charge in missing wife's death.

Barakat, M. (2017, August 1). Man gets life without parole for killing son for insurance. *Associated Press.*

Becker, I.S. (2018, October 26). A young "hustler" was fished from the Mississippi River in 1982. Now the case has taken a chilling turn. When a teenager was found lifeless in the Mississippi River, a New Orleans detective pointed to murder. Was he right? *Washington Post.*

Bever, L. (2018, September 13). A teen confessed to smothering his siblings, police say. His mom insists he's "not a monster;" the 14-year-old has been charged with murder in the deaths of his 2-year-old half-sister, Desiree McCartney, and his 11-month-old stepbrother, Nathaniel Ritz. *Washington Post.*

Bonvillian, C. (2018, September 4). Police: Woman charged with killing 2 baby daughters scoured internet for ways to kill. *Dayton Daily News.*

Bonvillian, C. (2019, March 19). N.C. man charged with killing second wife, "accidental" death of first wife. *Dayton Daily News.*

Brasch, B. (2018, March 25). AJC investigates cult founder in Marietta: Violent Florida cult leader was living the Cobb life. *Atlanta Journal-Constitution.*

Divine, M. (2019, November 19). Minnesota woman's death a mystery 4 decades later. *Associated Press.*

Donaldson, A. (2020, February 22). Mother of two missing kids will fight extradition, remain in jail. *Deseret Morning News.*

Eltman, F. (2017, September 16). Prosecutor renews interest in Long Island serial killer case. *Associated Press.*

Fieldstadt, E. (2019, July 18). Father charged with murder for driving sons with autism off L.A. picr. *NBC News.*

Fineout, G. (2018, December 15). Florida tale of infidelity and homicide ends with conviction. *Associated Press.*

Flynn, M. (2018, February 21). A man claimed his wife had been lost at sea. The FBI charged him with murder. *Washington Post.*

Flynn, M. (2020, February 6). His wife died in a house fire. His son was crushed under a truck. A jury finds it was all part of the plan. *Washington Post.*

Gambardello, J.A. (2019, July 14). Son held in killing after case reopened; natural causes had been cited in mother's January death. Then a relative came forward. *Philadelphia Inquirer.*

Harris, D. (2019, July 24). Death first ruled natural, but after funeral director findings police launch homicide investigation. *11 Alive*.

Hickman, H. (2019, October 8). Knoxville mom among victims of Samuel Little, most prolific serial killer in U.S. history. *Knoxville News Sentinel*.

Jany, L. (2018, February 7). Murder charges filed in death first thought to be accidental. *Star Tribune*.

Kennedy, M., and Schwartz, M. (2020, July 14). Former VA medical worker pleads guilty to murdering 7 patients in West Virginia. *NPR*.

Leader, A. (2019, May 21). Woman accused in death of newborn granted pretrial release. *Associated Press*.

Llamas, T. (2019, December 22). Eye drop poison plot; husband charged with murdering his wife. *ABC News*.

Logan, E. (2019, November 21). Man sentenced to 11 years for killing and hiding mentally disabled roommate in apartment wall. *Los Angeles Times*.

Moreno, I. (2018, February 25). Woman charged in 3 infant deaths in '80s. *Wisconsin State Journal*.

*Noticias Financieras*. (2019, July 30). One man said his truck fortuitously caught fire and killed his family: 10 years later he was arrested for murder.

O'Cain, P. (2019, June 18). Woman to be sentenced today in son's death. *Spokesman Review*.

Ransom, J. (2019, March 13). He wanted his wife's fortune. So he killed her, then tried framing his daughter. *New York Times*.

Repard, P. (2019, August 15). Zahau's sister offers $100,000 reward: Tips sought to help convict Shacknai in mansion death. *San Diego Union Tribune*.

Rojas, R. (2017, December 21). Woman who sabotaged her fiancé's kayak is released 5 months after guilty plea. *New York Times*.

Swenson, K. (2018, September 5). His wife said he died falling down the stairs. Police say she poisoned him with eye drops. *Washington Post*.

Swenson, K. (2019, March 6). Two sisters committed "the perfect murder," police say. A bizarre love triangle exposed the truth; authorities thought Anthony Tomaselli died of cancer and old age. The truth was much darker. *Washington Post*.

*Telegraph Herald*. (2020, May 6). Authorities: Manchester man arrested in 2004 killing.

Thompson, M. (2019, August 28). Michigan man accused of putting fatal dose of heroin in his wife's cereal. *CNN.com*.

Vincent, I., and Dorn, S. (2020, February 9). "Strangle" wounds point to "homicide." Forensics doc challenges city's ruling on woman's tragic chute fall. *New York Post*.

Vitello, B. (2019, July 17). Medical examiner: South Barrington woman's 2000 drowning death a homicide. *Chicago Daily Herald*.

Weiner, R. (2018, September 20). Woman, 63, pleads guilty to possessing ricin. *Washington Post*.

Weiner, R. (2019, April 13). Woman's death at home ruled a homicide. *Washington Post*.

Wheeler, K. (2018, February 15). Prosecutor: Stepfather disposed of toddler's body after child suffered fatal injury in 2002; defense attorney says defendant loved his stepson and didn't kill him. *City News Service*.

# Index

References to endnotes show both the page number and the note number (231n3).

First World War 76
food/drink tampering 69–72, 76
  *see also* product tampering
forensic dentistry 128
Foster, Carolyn 28
Foster, Thomas 28, 138
4chan 107, 108
Fox, J.A. 63, 86, 95, 120
framing other people 36, 70
Franklin, J. 112, 113
fraud 40
freak accidents 48, 62
Frei Montalva, Eduardo 80–81
Frieden, J. 96, 102
friends ("frenemies") 39–44
Frischknecht, F. 75, 76
frustration 15, 105
Frustration-Aggression Hypothesis 16–17
Fullerton, Maryann 38

**G**

"Gamergate" 109
Garbutt, Randolph 139
gender
  gender roles (traditional) 13, 23
  homicides 8
  medical settings 99
  physical power 13, 23
General Strain Theory 16–17
Geneva Protocol 76, 122
Genrich, James 43–44
Gilbert, Kristen 99–100
glanders 76
government and politics 74–89
Graham, Gwendolyn 94–97
Grand Junction, Colorado 43
"grassing"/"snitching" 121
Graswald, Angelika 144
Greydanus, D.E. 17, 18
Grimmie, Christina 104
guerrilla movements 78–79

**H**

hacking 107, 109–110, 111
hangings 6–7
Hansell, Jackie Rocket-Smart 58
Harris, Jason T. 133–134
Harry, Sandra 42
Harry Jr, Lewis Allen 42
Harvey, Donald 94
Hatfill, Steven 82, 83
Health Insurance Portability and
  Accountability Act (HIPAA) 93
healthcare 90–103
heart attacks/cardiac episodes 32, 33, 36, 48,
  49, 99, 100, 124
Heitzeg, N.A. 57
Heleker, Mark 57
Henrichsen, J. 108

Henthorn, Harold 37
Henthorn, Toni (Bertolet) 37
hero, wanting to be a 100–101
Hess, Amanda 110
hiding in plain sight 15
high profile people 105–107
higher education 59–60
history of abuse 23–27
hoaxes 65, 82
home-care professionals 96–97, 102
homicides
  age of victims 9
  gender 8
  motives 10
  relationship perpetrator-victim 9–10
  in US death statistics 3
Horowitz, J.M. 118, 119
hospitals, deaths in 90
Human Rights Watch 66
Hunsucker, Joshua 136–137
Hurd, Elaine 135–136

**I**

illness statistics 90
impetus for reclassifications 6–7
indirect aggression 18
"indirect violence" 18
individualism 13
inequality gaps 11–12, 118
initiation rituals 94
injections, killings via 85, 98, 101
innocent people, convictions of 125–126
intelligence services 80
  *see also* Central Intelligence Agency (CIA)
intention
  firearm injuries 92
  intent to murder 29, 30
  malevolence in hospitals 92
"inter-criminal victimization" 17
international law 122–123
intimate partner violence 23–26, 123
Ivins, Bruce 82–83

**J**

Jacobs, B.A. 17
janitors 58
Japan 84
Johnson & Johnson 68–69
Johnston, M. 127
jokes/pranks 71, 111
Jones, Genene 100–101
Jones, Tieray 143

**K**

Kaczynski, Theodore 86–87, 122
Karlsen, Karl 131–132
Kedrowitz, Nickalas 141
Keel, Rexford Lynn 137
Khan, Urooj 32–33